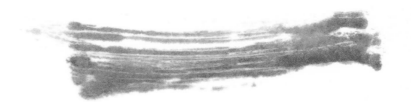

EARLY BLACK WRITERS

General Editors
PAUL EDWARDS
and
DAVID DABYDEEN

'Our Children Free and Happy'

*Letters from Black Settlers in Africa
in the 1790s*

edited by
CHRISTOPHER FYFE
with a contribution by
CHARLES JONES

EDINBURGH UNIVERSITY PRESS

© Edinburgh University Press 1991
22 George Square, Edinburgh

Typeset in Linotron Garamond
by Nene Phototypesetters,
Northampton, and
printed in Great Britain by
Hartnolls Limited, Bodmin, Cornwall

British Library Cataloguing
in Publication Data
'Our children free and happy':
Letters from Black settlers in
Africa in the 1790s. –
(Early black writers series)
I. Fyfe, Christopher II. Series
966.4

ISBN 0 7486 0270 4 (cased)

Contents

Preface

The story of the Nova Scotian settlers in Sierra Leone has been told many times. Two comprehensive studies appeared in 1976: James Walker's *The Black Loyalists*, and Ellen Gibson Wilson's *The Loyal Blacks*. The Nova Scotian settlers also figure in some detail in the historical works listed in the *Selected Bibliography* (on page 105), and Yema Lucilda Hunter has told their story with great insight in her novel *Road to Freedom*. Bearing this in mind I have contributed only a brief introduction, setting out the story for those unfamiliar with it, without incorporating documentary references. Those interested in studying it further can do so from the books listed in the *Selected Bibliography*.

The value of this publication has been greatly enhanced by the inclusion of a contribution by Professor Charles Jones of the University of Edinburgh on the style of English used by the settlers.

I am grateful to Ellen Gibson Wilson for generously lending me photocopies of some of the documents to work from. I must also record my thanks to the owners of the originals for permission to reproduce them – to the British Library (Manuscript Collections), the Special Collections (Sierra Leone Collection) of the University Library, University of Illinois at Chicago, and the Public Record Office. But above all I thank my dear old friend Paul Edwards who suggested to me that the Nova Scotian letters be published as a volume in his Early Black Writers series and encouraged and helped me to edit them.

In the documents the settlers tell their story themselves in their own words. Across two centuries we hear members of a self-liberated black community defending their rights and expressing their feelings in their own way. They have been reproduced as written, without editorial interference, to carry the authentic sound of their voices to present-day readers.

CHRISTOPHER FYFE
Centre of African Studies
University of Edinburgh

Nova Scotian Settlers' Documents

Introduction

The documents in this collection were written in the late eighteenth century by black people who had liberated themselves from slavery. During the American War of Independence the British authorities offered freedom to slaves who left their owners and joined the British forces. Tens of thousands seized the opportunity and escaped to the British lines. Eventually some 3,000 men and women – for women too left their owners, bringing their children with them – were taken away to settle as free people in the British colony of Nova Scotia.

Freedom for them meant living their own lives in economic independence on their own land. They saw land as the guarantee of their security. But the land grants they were promised were rarely forthcoming. Slavery was still legal in Nova Scotia and they feared that without land they might find themselves slaves again. So in 1791 Thomas Peters, a middle-aged millwright, who had freed himself from slavery in North Carolina and then served as a sergeant in the British army, courageously crossed the Atlantic to London to seek redress. He returned with the offer of a new home for them in Africa, in Sierra Leone, under the sponsorship of the Sierra Leone Company, a commercial company founded in London by opponents of the slave trade, who were establishing a settlement for free blacks on the west coast of Africa.

Some feared to embark and remained in a life of abject poverty and humiliation in Nova Scotia (where their descendants survive today). But nearly 2,000 accepted the offer of a new life in Africa. For all of them it was a voyage to the home of their ancestors. For some it was a return to the continent of their birth – and for a few it was even a return to the very country, Sierra Leone, whence they had been shipped across the Atlantic as slaves.

1

The documents assembled in this volume illustrate their growing disillusionment in their new home, where they became increasingly estranged from the directors and employees of the Sierra Leone Company. It was a dialogue of the deaf. On one side were well-meaning whites who saw the black settlers as a means of introducing what they perceived as 'the Blessings of Industry and Civilization' into Africa. On the other were the black settlers, hoping to live out in Africa, in their own way, the life of freedom denied them in America, 'to make our children free and happy' (Document 19).

Neither could fully share, if indeed fully understand, the other's objectives and priorities. Over the following decade the settlers' grievances built up (as these documents detail) until eventually in 1800 some of them rose in armed rebellion.

The story of the Sierra Leone settlement began some years before their arrival in Africa. It originated in London with Granville Sharp, a single-minded visionary who was responsible for forcing the English courts to declare in 1772 that a former slave could not be sent back to slavery in the colonies. At the end of the American War of Independence there was a sudden influx of self-liberated slaves into Britain, chiefly London. Sharp persuaded the British government to accept financial responsibility for them, and to send them in 1787 to a new home in Sierra Leone – the country of their own choice. Their decision to settle in Sierra Leone in 1787, and the subsequent choice made by the Nova Scotian settlers to make their homes there, may be taken as the first practical manifestation of Pan-Africanism.

Sharp drew up a constitution for 'The Province of Freedom', as he called it. It was to be a self-governing community whose members would choose their own government. So immediately on arrival in Sierra Leone the black settlers elected one of themselves as governor. But they had arrived at the onset of the long rainy season, and this first rainy season was a disaster. Most fell ill and about a third of them died.

And though the Temne rulers who owned the land welcomed them at first, they unwisely quarrelled with their nearest neighbour, King Jimmy, who drove them away and burnt down their town.

Meanwhile, in Britain, a campaign against the slave trade was starting. A group of its members decided to take over Sharp's abandoned settlement and revive it with new settlers as a commercial company, the Sierra Leone Company. Their aim was two-fold: to replace the slave trade by trade in vegetable produce, and to introduce the 'Blessings of Industry and Civilization' into Africa. But the settlement was to be run by a board of directors in London. It was no longer to be the self-governing Province of Freedom that Sharp had intended. It was they who offered Thomas Peters a home for the Nova Scotian blacks in Africa, and he returned across the Atlantic in 1791 with their offer.

The people were scattered in small communities across Nova Scotia and New Brunswick within which they were forming themselves into cohesive religious congregations. Freedom had brought them freedom to join the Christian churches from which many had been excluded when they were slaves. They flocked to be baptised, and the white religious authorities provided schools for their children. But the white churches were unwilling to open their doors to black Christians. So, in the wake of a Methodist 'awakening' that was sweeping Nova Scotia, black preachers founded congregations of their own. As well as Methodist congregations there were Baptists, and congregations of the Countess of Huntingdon's Connexion (or Huntingdonians), an independent church which had broken away from the Church of England under the leadership of the Countess of Huntingdon. She sent a black minister to Nova Scotia to preach to the blacks and they founded their own Huntingdonian churches.

The churches were a focus of loyalty for the people and gave them their own leaders. Moreover, as James Walker has convincingly demonstrated, the churches gave them the sense of a black identity, quite distinct from the white community in Nova Scotia or in Sierra Leone. Also, as their writings show, their churches gave them much of their vocabulary and verbal imagery.

A young naval officer, John Clarkson, whose brother Thomas, a leading figure in the campaign against the slave trade and slavery, was one of the Sierra Leone Company directors, was sent to Nova Scotia to organise the emigration. Clarkson combined practical efficiency with passionately felt emotions. He was deeply moved by the wretched plight of the black people and committed himself whole-heartedly to them. They in return responded to his commitment and gave him their unwavering confidence and affection, seeing him as a Moses come to lead them out from the land of bondage (Document 28).

He quickly learnt that freedom for them consisted above all in a secure title to a piece of land, to make them and their children independent, free to live lives of their own. They feared the imposition of any permanent charge on the land, like the quit–rents they were charged in Nova Scotia. So from the pulpit of the Methodist church in Birchtown, the main black settlement, he promised them land in Sierra Leone free of quit–rents.

Here he went beyond his instructions. After he had left London the directors had drawn up terms explicitly offering land subject to a small annual quit–rent. This he had not been told. More than anything else his unauthorised promise was to sour future relations between the settlers and the Sierra Leone Company.

Prospective settlers flocked to join Clarkson in Halifax, braving the hostility of the white population who resented the loss of labour. Pastors brought their congregations. David George who, as a slave, had been pastor of Silver Bluff Baptist Church in South Carolina, the first black church in North America, brought his Baptist congregations. Moses Wilkinson, the blind and lame Methodist pastor in Birchtown, whose pulpit Clarkson had spoken from, brought his, as did a Huntingdonian pastor, Cato Perkins. Another Methodist preacher, Boston King, was stirred by the opportunity of preaching the Christian message in Africa. Though he had prospered as a free man and was earning a comfortable living in Nova Scotia, he volunteered for Sierra Leone. Richard Crankapone (or Corankeapon), who was to be a prominent figure in Sierra Leone, led four men three hundred miles on foot from New Brunswick to Halifax through the snowy forests.

They were, as Clarkson always rightly insisted, outstandingly good potential settlers – enterprising, self-reliant men and women who had freed themselves from slavery. Some had served in the armed forces (and brought their muskets with them), some had specialised trades. Some could read and write. Those who were church pastors and elders were articulate and had learnt how to lead and care for their congregations. All were ready to face unknown perils for the sake of a better life of freedom.

The cost of the emigration was paid by the British government in recognition of their loyalty to Britain and their service in the war. Clarkson organised them into companies under their own elected captains who were responsible for discipline on board the fifteen transport ships. Meanwhile he had to deal with their numerous problems and anxieties as they awaited departure (Documents 1–3). Before sailing, each household head was issued with a certificate granting him or her land in Sierra Leone, and eventually on 15 January 1792 they sailed for Africa.

The Sierra Leone Company's settlement was conceived on a substantial scale. £235,280 was subscribed by shareholders as capital, to create an urban commercial centre, 'Freetown', surrounded by farmlands. The settlers were to receive rations for an initial period, free medical care and free schooling for their children. In return for this considerable outlay the directors of the Company hoped for an eventual profit from produce grown on their own plantations or exchanged for imported consumer goods with the neighbouring peoples.

But their plans were poorly executed. When the settlers arrived from Nova Scotia the settlement was in confusion. The directors had sent out over a hundred white employees, supervised by a council of eight with Clarkson as superintendent. The site was uncleared, the councillors and other officials still living on board ships in the harbour. Clarkson had no authority over his fellow councillors who did what they chose, issuing contradictory orders and quarrelling with one another. At last, after nearly five months, in reply to his urgent demands, the directors disbanded the council and gave him full powers as governor with a subordinate council of two.

Meanwhile the Nova Scotian settlers (as they continued to be called) landed, cleared the site and began putting up houses and planting vegetable gardens. They tended to locate according to their shipboard companies, sticking together under their own leaders. Then the heavy rains began with the same disastrous effects as on the first settlement. Malaria and dysentery broke out and about a hundred died. Two-thirds of the whites also died and many of the rest went home. Clarkson was constantly ill, driven into fits of hysterical weeping with loss of memory, by the insubordination of his white colleagues and the incessant demands made on him by the settlers (Documents 4–13).

Having promised them land he tried to make land survey a priority. But the disorganised white officials, the rains and the heavy mortality all slowed it up. When the rations granted for the initial months ceased, the people were still unable to support themselves on their own land, as had been intended. Instead they had to work for the Company on public works for wages. Inevitably, having suffered all their lives under white oppression, they were suspicious of any threat to what they believed to be their rights. For, like their former American owners, they believed they were entitled to inalienable rights – the rights they had been denied in slave-owning America and had come to Africa to enjoy.

They set down what they saw as their rights in a petition submitted to Clarkson by Henry Beverhout, one of the Methodist preachers, on behalf of his company (Document 7). It demonstrated clearly that they understood the political concepts and vocabulary of contemporary Britain and America and could use them to maintain their own interests. It also illustrates (as do most of their letters and petitions) that they were familiar with the formal style of submitting petitions to authority usual at the period.

In it they made clear that they regarded themselves as free agents, entitled to make their own political decisions. They expressed willingness to be governed by the laws of England but only on condition that people of their own colour were given some participation, including the right to have their own juries and police constables.

This Clarkson immediately introduced. Henceforth all law cases were tried before settler juries. And John Cuthbert, a Baptist preacher, was appointed marshal to enforce writs and summon juries. When he went on a visit to England Richard Crankapone succeeded him.

What Clarkson would not tolerate was a rival. Thomas Peters, whose initiative had originally brought the settlers to Sierra Leone, had no more authority there than any of the other captains, and felt wounded at being excluded from recognition and eclipsed by Clarkson. Though not a preacher, he attended the nightly prayer meetings and urged the people to recognise him as their head. Clarkson subtly thwarted him, covertly winning over his supporters and undermining his influence. In June Peters fell ill and died, leaving Clarkson undisputed leader. Even so, he and the other officials were constantly aware of the people's growing dissatisfaction and their suspicion of white motives.

In December he went home on sick leave, intending to marry and return. His two councillors, William Dawes and Zachary Macaulay, were left in charge. In addition, local government was introduced on lines proposed for the original settlement by Granville Sharp. Every ten freeholders, men

and women, elected a tythingman and every ten tythingmen a
hundredor (titles Sharp had picked up from ancient Anglo-
Saxon usage), to settle disputes and keep order as constables.
They could also propose laws to the governor's council which
had ultimate control, subject to the authority of the directors
of the Sierra Leone Company in London.

Before leaving, Clarkson preached two long, emotional farewell sermons, begging them to accept frustrations patiently
and reprehending the 'improper notions of liberty' that
were leading some of them to go against authority. Some
walked out of the church in temporary offence. But most
grieved at his departure and begged him to return (Document
14). And in future years even those most virulent against the
Company's government were to turn to him for support as
the one white man they believed they could trust (Documents
18–24, 27–34).

It had been assumed that the settlers would support themselves on the land in Sierra Leone, growing their own crops.
But much of the land round Freetown was unsuited to
farming – steep, wooded mountain slopes with little depth of
soil. Nor was there enough to supply everyone with their
promised farm allocations. Surveying this unpromising
terrain went slowly. They blamed Dawes, Clarkson's well-
meaning but unsympathetic successor, fearing always that
without land they would again be reduced to being slaves.
Meanwhile they could only gain a livelihood working for the
Company for wages that barely sufficed to buy provisions
from the Company's store. Always suspicious of white
motives, they saw dependence as the path back to slavery.

But in London it was taken for granted that work for the
Company was work towards abolishing the slave trade and
regenerating Africa. The directors saw the Nova Scotians as
collaborators in their great enterprise, but collaborators who
needed guidance and control. They found it difficult to
take seriously accusations that they, outspoken campaigners

against the slave trade, were trying to reduce their protégés to slavery, and tended to assume that the settlers' protests were activated either by ignorance or misunderstanding or else by disloyalty and subversion.

Dawes also stirred up resentment by trying to reserve for the Sierra Leone Company waterfront land already occupied by Luke Jordan, a Methodist preacher, and his company which Clarkson had promised they should be allowed to retain (Document 23). Called 'Brothers Street', after the ship on which the company had crossed the Atlantic, it became known to the white officials as 'Discontented Row' (and is today Malamah Thomas Street).

Their grievances mounted and they sent two delegates, Cato Perkins and Isaac Anderson, to London to ask the directors for redress and for Clarkson to return (Documents 18, 19). Perkins, the Huntingdonian pastor, was an outspoken preacher whose theology stressed personal freedom and judgement. He maintained that he and his congregation were inspired directly by the Holy Spirit and needed no man-made mediation. Anderson, a free born man, a carpenter by trade, had served in the British army against the Americans. He lived in Brothers Street, and during the early months had had a violent altercation with Clarkson for which he subsequently apologised.

But the directors now turned against Clarkson and dismissed him. They were frightened of his promises to the people and saw that his views and theirs were incompatible – that he would always interpret instructions according to his own deeply-held feelings rather than to the letter of their intentions. Bitterly hurt, he abandoned his connexion with Africa and took up a business career in Suffolk. He was not allowed to see Perkins and Anderson, who returned home without any redress from the directors (Documents 20–22). And though over the next five years he received regular letters of complaint from settlers (Documents 23–4, 27–34), loyalty to his former employers, despite their treatment of him, restrained him from taking up their cause actively.

Relations between the Company's officials and the people began to polarise: Macaulay could even refer in his journal to a black preacher as being 'of the white party'. When the Company's storeship, the *York*, caught fire in Freetown harbour none of the settlers would go to help extinguish it, alleging that there might be gunpowder on board. Indeed some rejoiced at what they interpreted as God's judgement on their oppressors. In London this could only seem ingratitude for all the Company had done for them.

Dawes and Macaulay (who in later years in Britain was to be in the forefront of the campaigns against the slave trade and slavery) were ready enough to uphold the settlers' rights as British subjects. When three white sailors killed a duck belonging to a settler Macaulay had them tried by a settler jury, and sentenced one to be publicly flogged by the settler appointed to administer floggings, and the others fined. But he insisted, as indeed Clarkson had, that they must be obedient to the Company's authority.

Slavery was illegal in the colony, but beyond it was still legal. Slave ships legally loaded with slaves sailed regularly down the estuary past Freetown. Nor could slave traders be kept out of the colony. In 1794 two settlers employed by the Company threatened a visiting slave trader who had spoken to them abusively with violence and Macaulay, fearing reprisals, dismissed them from the Company's service (Document 23). The hundredors and tythingmen protested and raised other grievances. When Macaulay rejected their protest there was uproar. Richard Crankapone was beaten up and crowds, including some women, took to the streets and threatened Macaulay's house. Fearing an attack, he gave arms to the Company's employees and a few of the settlers he could rely on.

After two days of uproar, during which the Company's office was plundered, the excitement died down. Macaulay (whose persuasive logic contrasted with Clarkson's emotional rhetoric) issued an address pointing out that the Company, whatever its faults, was their only source of protection in

Africa, and offering to send anyone dissatisfied with its rule back to Nova Scotia free of charge, chartering a ship to take them. No one accepted his offer. The hundredors and tythingmen then arrested the rioters who were sent to England for trial, as the Company had no jurisdiction to try serious offences.

War between Britain and France began in 1793 and was to last intermittently for over twenty years. It not only ended the Company's hopes of profit but brought financial disaster. From now on the Company's ships were regularly captured by the French. Worse, in September 1794, a French squadron attacked Freetown. As the colony was virtually without defences Macaulay surrendered immediately to the seven heavily armed French warships confronting them. The crews then landed and looted the town, destroying everything they could and eventually burning it down, while the settlers sheltered in the bush or in nearby Temne villages.

When the French had gone they returned and rebuilt the town (on the street plan that still survives in central Freetown). But in this resettlement period a new disagreement arose. During the confusion some had helped themselves to goods belonging to the Company. Macaulay asked to have them back, offering 20 per cent of the value instead. Little was returned, so he drew up a declaration for everyone to sign, stating that they had none of the Company's property in their possession, and denied free medical services and schooling to those who refused. Some of the settlers felt this a bitter grievance (Documents 24–26).

Some even suggested that the French invasion had brought the Company's rule to an end and that its laws were no longer valid (Document 25). Luke Jordan's Methodist congregation acquired land along the shore west of Freetown at Pirates' (or Cockle) Bay from the Temne ruler Prince George, where they could go and live free of the Company's jurisdiction (Documents 28–30). For though in later years the settlers were to distance themselves from their African neighbours, at this period they were normally on good terms with the neighbouring rulers. Indeed some saw them as potential allies against the Company.

Despite these contentions the colony re-established itself. The Company could no longer afford a large payroll so the people turned to their own resources. Those who had been allotted accessible fertile land began farming, chiefly for subsistence. Others built boats and traded for produce with the neighbouring peoples, or opened up shops or set up as craftsmen. Profits were invested in building wooden framed houses, styled on the pioneer North American pattern, to live in or let to white officials. Thus they established the economic base of Freetown's future prosperity – import-export trade and investment in house-property.

A high proportion of householders were women without husbands. Their independent status was recognised. They received allotments of land, and voted in the elections for hundredors and tythingmen until 1797 when they were excluded. But though excluded from direct political activity, they established a hold on the economy. Three of the first six retail traders to open shops were women. Like the men they invested their profits in houses, and within a few years women owned some of the best properties in Freetown.

The hundredors and tythingmen met regularly as a local parliament and made laws approved by the governor and council. They fixed the price of bread and introduced a road tax, making all adult landholders, men and women, supply six days' labour a year on the roads or commute with a fine. They granted a divorce to a man whose wife had remained in Nova Scotia. When a militia was organised the officers were elected, and Macaulay forced white officials without military experience to serve under the experienced black captains.

Regular use was made of the law courts where the settlers' own juries gave the verdicts. Their own constables enforced public order. The preachers and elders too kept their congregations under discipline and saw to it that public behaviour conformed to the norms of Christian respectability. They assembled regularly for worship, some of them daily, and observed Sunday strictly. Thus whatever feelings they might have against the Company and its officials, the settlers constituted a basically peaceable, law-abiding community.

The Company's terms to the Nova Scotians had stipulated payment of an annual quit–rent for their land (see p. 4 above). Now needing to raise revenue to offset the losses of war, the directors sent instructions in 1796 requiring payment of what was in effect an annual land tax of one shilling per acre. In London a quit–rent seemed a small and reasonable demand to make from people for whom the Company had paid out so much. To the settlers it seemed a threat to their independence. They argued that once the land was subject to tax they risked being evicted for non-payment and hence, as they saw it, they and their children might be reduced to the status of landless slaves. It was also a breach of Clarkson's promise which they remembered as, 'before God that they should have no quit–rent to pay'. (Quoted in retrospect in Minutes of Council, 17 November 1801, Public Record Office CO270/6.)

From the Company's side the Nova Scotians seemed to be unreasonable and ungrateful. From the Nova Scotian side the Company seemed to be depriving them of the liberty they had won for themselves in America and had come to Africa to enjoy.

To reinforce the Company's claims, legal proceedings were brought to evict Luke Jordan and his people from the contested Brothers Street. But the settler jury found in Jordan's favour (Document 31). Public emotion was also stirred by rumours spread by two white preachers – a former schoolmaster and a Baptist missionary – that the government meant to close down the Nova Scotian churches. At the elections for hundredors and tythingmen at the end of the year most of those elected were active opponents of the government. They included Jordan, Anderson and their neighbour Nathaniel Snowball. A few months later Snowball led about a dozen families out of the colony to settle under his governorship at Pirates' Bay (Document 32).

Law-abiding as they were, ready to pay the road tax they had voted for themselves and accept other civic duties, they would not tolerate quit–rents. As they saw it, the land was theirs and paying a quit–rent made it not theirs but the Company's. The hundredors and tythingmen protested formally, maintaining that they would never have left Nova Scotia if they had known it was payable (Document 35). Some of the pastors threatened to excommunicate any member of his congregation who paid. There was even talk of seizing power from the Company by force with the help of neighbouring Temne rulers – talk Macaulay quieted by threatening anyone who tried to do so with the gallows.

However, as no attempt was made to collect quit–rents most of the people gradually reverted to their normally peaceful state. At the elections in 1798 less militant representatives were chosen including even one of the Company's white officials.

The Temne and other coastal peoples had known white traders for centuries. Established usages had grown up to regulate their relations. Traders paid recognised rents and other payments to the rulers of the towns they settled in (their 'landlords') for permission to trade. The landlord and his people retained sovereignty and ownership of the land. When the landlord died the trader had to negotiate a new agreement with his successor.

But the Sierra Leone settlement had been established by a treaty which alienated sovereignty over the ceded land. The Temne rulers, who had put their names to it without being able to read it, had assumed it was a treaty of the familiar kind. Yet when they demanded their rights as landlords the Company's officials refused them, maintaining that the land was no longer theirs. Hence relations between the Colony government and its neighbours, originally friendly, gradually deteriorated.

The Company's directors who were now faced with commercial ruin by the war against France, sought financial support from the British government. In Jamaica a community of self-liberated 'Maroons' (as runaway slaves were styled there) had been involved in rebellion against the government and had been shipped off the island to Nova Scotia. The directors agreed to take them as settlers in Sierra Leone in return for a government subvention, a small garrison of British soldiers and a royal charter of justice to give the Company unquestionable jurisdiction in the colony.

Meanwhile in 1798 they again demanded quit–rents. The people showed their reaction at the December elections when they chose staunch defenders of their rights. The hundredors included Isaac Anderson, their former delegate to London, and Ansel Zizer (Document 13). The tythingmen chose as their chairman and deputy chairman two men who were to become increasingly prominent – James Robertson (or Robinson), an elderly shopkeeper with a grievance over a lawsuit he had failed to win, and Nathaniel Wansey who farmed on the hill above the town (later Tower Hill). When orders came from London that only children whose parents had paid the quit–rent would be educated free of charge the children were withdrawn from the Company's school. Anxious though parents were to have their children educated, it could not be at the price of a quit–rent.

A new governor took over from Macaulay during 1799, Thomas Ludlam, a scholarly-minded twenty-three year old without previous administrative experience. He made no attempt to collect quit–rents. But many people remained suspicious and anxious to safeguard their rights. Robertson and Wansey requested that the hundredors and tythingmen be allowed to appoint two justices of the peace and a judge. The request was refused. Nevertheless they made the three judicial appointments, Anderson being one of them. Ludlam turned down the appointments and referred their request to London.

Asking to appoint judges went beyond what most of the settlers wanted. They already had their own juries who could, and sometimes did, give verdicts against the government (see p. 13 above), and were content to accept the Company's officials as judges. The Methodist preachers, strong against quit–rents, declined to give support to those who were now going on to question the Company's right to rule.

In September the hundredors and tythingmen resolved that the settlers were the proprietors of the colony and that no foreigner might settle in it without their consent (Document 37). Ludlam refused to accept the resolution, but acted cautiously, looking forward to the arrival of the promised detachment of soldiers and charter of justice to sustain his authority. But in December he announced publicly that the directors had turned down the request to choose judges. At the subsequent elections Robertson, Anderson and Zizer were among the hundredors and Wansey chairman of the tythingmen.

Soon after, the captain of a slave ship quarrelled with King Tom, a Temne ruler who lived nearby (on the peninsula which still bears his name) over the payment of anchorage dues. Ludlam offered to mediate, promising the captain safe conduct if he came to the negotiations unarmed. But when he arrived a body of settlers turned out and threatened to hand him over to King Tom unless he made immediate payment. The captain had to pay (the Company subsequently compensated him for the enforced breach of faith), while Ludlam was publicly exposed to humiliation and shown to be powerless.

Still temporizing, he asked the hundredors and tythingmen to draw up a statement detailing in what ways they felt themselves injured. In reply they instanced various grievances 'to show that we cannot get justice from the white people' (Document 38). At a subsequent session they chose Robertson as judge and John Cuthbert, once a supporter of the government but increasingly its opponent, as justice of the peace. Ludlam again refused to accept these appointments and issued a long address answering their complaints and warning them that when the royal charter arrived the Company's authority would be backed by the British crown. Only a few turned up to hear his address read. At the end Robertson rose and declared that no courts of law were to sit until new laws had been made.

His words signified that he and his associates no longer considered the colony to be under the Company's government and were preparing their own. The tythingmen expelled those who opposed them and put in their own supporters. Allegedly there was some wild talk of sending the whites out to sea in an oarless boat. Then in September 1800 the hundredors and tythingmen issued their own code of laws, signed by Robertson, Zizer, Anderson and Wansey (Document 39). It fixed prices, specified fines for a variety of criminal offences, and gave power to scrutinise the Company's claims for debt. The governor and council were to confine themselves in future to the Company's affairs, 'and all that come from Nova Scotia shall be under this law or quit the place'. A subsequent paper proclaimed the laws to be in force (Document 40).

As this constituted rebellion Ludlam assembled the Company's officials and a few of the settlers he could count on at Fort Thornton, the fortified governor's house built above the town after the French invasion, and gave them arms. Crankapone, as marshal, went with a small group of constables to arrest the signatories of the proposed laws. There was a skirmish in which the constables opened fire and several people were wounded. Robertson was captured. Zizer gave himself up. Anderson and Wansey escaped and next day gathered their followers under Anderson's leadership at a bridge to the east of Freetown.

Only about fifty of the three hundred or so householders joined Isaac Anderson. Most remained quietly in Freetown. It was one thing to refuse to pay quit–rents – another to take arms against the government and to subject themselves to

Anderson and Wansey's laws. John Cuthbert had accepted an unauthorised judgeship, but when it came to fighting he offered to mediate. So did Cato Perkins, though most of the rebels were from his congregation. Even so, not more than about thirty settlers could be counted on to fight for the Company.

Anderson sent a message to Ludlam threatening that if he did not release those held as captives he must turn any women and children out of the fort – implying that he must expect a fight (Document 41). King Tom also sent a message to say that if the dispute was not settled within a few days he would come and settle it himself. This was indeed alarming news for Ludlam in view of his recent public humiliation.

All changed dramatically when a ship anchored and proved to be the transport carrying the Maroons with a detachment of soldiers on board. In their Jamaican homeland the Maroons had been under contract to the government to track down escaped slaves and were happy to help their new government suppress a rebellion. Most of the rebels were rounded up with little fighting. Anderson took refuge with a Temne ruler but was given up. Wansey and a few others escaped.

To avoid protracted legal proceedings, a military court was constituted by the newly arrived officers, and thirty-one were sentenced to be banished from the colony for life. Five, including James Robertson and John Cuthbert, were sent to Gorée (Senegal), then a British colony, and the rest, including Ansel Zizer, across the estuary to the Bulom Shore. Eventually they were amnestied and some, including Zizer, returned to the colony. The banished rebels included Henry Washington, once slave to George Washington, but less successful in rebellion than his former owner.

Isaac Anderson was reserved for trial at the sessions constituted under the new charter of justice, with two others, Joseph Waring, and Francis Patrick who from his early days in the colony had made himself obnoxious to authority. Waring's indictment was thrown out by the grand jury.

Anderson and Patrick were convicted of felony and hanged (Document 41).

Wansey and a few others remained at large. King Tom, now alarmed by the arrival of British soldiers, decided to attack the colony with Wansey's help. But two successive invasions failed. Instead King Tom and his people were driven off the northern shore of the peninsula which was then annexed to the colony. Wansey was eventually captured. His fate is not indicated in the surviving records.

With the new charter of justice the settlers lost their political voice. The hundredors and tythingmen were abolished. But they kept their jury rights and the quit–rent was abandoned. The bankrupt Company struggled on until 1808 when it handed over the colony to the British crown.

Under the British crown Sierra Leone was integrated into the campaign to suppress the slave trade, which had been made illegal in 1807. Freetown became a base for the British anti-slave trade naval squadron. When slave ships were captured by the navy the slaves were brought there, freed and settled in the colony. Within a few years the Nova Scotians were far outnumbered by the influx of thousands of freed people. They survived as a small, disappointed elite, still preserving tenaciously their separate identity. A few women from among the original settlers lived on until the 1870s. Some of their descendants are still in Freetown today.

Neither the Sierra Leone Company nor the Nova Scotians had seen their dream fulfilled. The 'Blessings of Industry and Civilization' the Company introduced had deprived the Temne of their land and provoked the Nova Scotians into rebellion. The settlers had found a new home, better than what they left in Nova Scotia, but without the kind of independence they had dreamed of, and had expressed their longing for in their letters and petitions.

The Documents

1. Birchtown People's Petition

To the Honble. Mr Clarkson Agent to the Sierra Leona Society. Whereas a Number of us Formerly Where Inhabitants of Birch Town near Shelburne Nova Scotia,But now intending under your Inspection to imbarque to Sierra Leona – Would Therefore humbly Solicit that on our arrival You will be pleased to settle us as near as Possible To the Inhabitants of Preston,as they and us Are intimately acquaint'd – so in order to Render us Unanimous,would be glad to be As Nearly Connected as possible when the Tract Or Tracts of Land shall be Laid out,humbly Relying up on your Interest in this matter,and In Compliance with this request will be bound To Pray ———

2. Thomas Peters and David Edmon, 23 December 1791

halefax   december the 23 1791

the humbel petion of the Black pepel lying in mr wisdoms Store Called the anoplus[1] Compnay humbely bag that if it is Consent to your honer as it is the larst Christmas day that we ever shall see in the amaraca that it may please your honer to grant us one days alowance of frish Beef for a Christmas diner that if it is agreabel to you and the rest of the Gentlemon to whom it may Consern

thomas petus
david Edmon[2]

3. Peter Richardson, 12 January 1792

Dear Sir the Ill behaviour Of Some Of the People that Went Against Orders Not Agreeable to the Rules Of the Law for One Of Our Woman Goes by the Name Of Sally Pone Mentions Some Expression that Other People May take Some holt And do As She has Done

23

And Said for She Says that she do not Care for You and I
Nor for Any Of the laws thatt Is made by Your Orders
for Sir this Morning There was some Of the People thatt
did not behave And did what was not Agreeable to the
Rules of Our Law and we was Exammining Of them and
this Woman Sally Pone came in when we was
Exammining them And She say what i have mention
Obove And not Only but Call us a pack of Deavils And
Mention many Expressions that was very Scandilous
And we Egreed to lett You know thatt She may be
Justifyed Acording to the Rules of the Law

Peter Richardson   Mr William Clarkson Esqr
On board of the Mary   Of his Magisty Navy
1 Syman Addams   Halifax
2 Warrick francies
3 John Prince
4 franck Patrick
5 George Black
Was in Preasant When theese Words was Mention by
Sally Pone

4. Susana Smith, 12 May 1792

Sierra Leone May 12th 1792
Sir I your hum bel Servent begs the faver of your
Excelence to See if you will Pleas to Let me hav Som
Sope for I am in great want of Som I hav not had aney
Since I hav bin to this plais I hav bin Sick and I want to
git Som Sope verry much to wash my family Clos for we
ar not fit to be Sean for dirt

     your hum   Susana Smith
     bel Servet

5. Richard Dickson, 15 May 1792

Sir

May it please your Excellencey – as you was speaking concerning the free School if your honour thinks proproper To begin I have got a yong man that is agreeable to take part of the children To school them and would be glad to know What you will allow him to school them Pr year as I think him capable of the Place we have appointed for him ———

I am sir yous Richard Dickson[1]
of Capt Perkins Company
Brig Betsey ——— Free Town May 15th 1792

6. Daniel Cary, 16 June 1792

Sir

I have wrote you these few Lines to informed you that I should wished to get married this afternoon if it is not unconvenient to you to do it for me from

your Servt

Dannail Cary

Freetown
June 16th

7. Beverhout Company, 26 June 1792

June the 26 1792
to his Excelency John Clarkson govener of the new Setlement of Saraleon and the tarataras theurin depending and sofourth – first the pepel of our Companey Consesents to the wagers that your honer proposul that is to work for two Shillens per day as long as we drowr our provsions

secon we are all willing to be govern by the laws of england in full but we donot Consent to gave it in to

your honer hands with out haven aney of our own
Culler in it –

therd thear is non of us wold wish for your honer to go
way and leave us hear but your will be pleased to rember
what your honer told the fiepel in a maraca at Shelburn
that is whoever Came to Saraleon wold be free and
should have a law and when theur war aney trial thear
should by a jurey of both white and black and all should
be equel so we Consideren all this think that we have a
wright to Chuse men that we think proper for to act for
us in a reasnenble manner

forth we are all willing to hold to your honer own word
and to the hen bill that we have got thear is not one of us
but is willing to hold to the hand bill[1]

fifly Sir we think it verey hard that your honer insist
upon our paying for what is taken up in the Stores at this
present for we expected to pay in the produse of our
lands a Coarden to the desiers of the Saraleon
Companey in england and we are thank full to them for
theur good desin we have no reasen to think but thear
intenion is to make us hapy and we all gave them thanks
for thear goodnes to us and pray that god will bles the
Saraleon Companey in england and will prosper them in
thear undertaken wherther we stand or fall

Six we are all willing to your honer preposuls that is to
have Constable a pinted in every street for to kepen pece

Seventh we wish for pece if posable we can but to gave
all out of our hands we cannot your honer know that we
can have laws and ragerlations among our self and be
Consirent with the laws of england because we have seen
it in all the parts whear eaver we have being

Sir we do not mene to take the law in our hands by no
meanes but to have your honer approbation for we own
you to be our had and govener

[The last page of the original is missing. Clarkson's copy
in his diary (26 December 1792) goes on:]

& we will be as good as our word to you in Halifax: we
honour you for the many kindnesses that we received
from you & we are willing to stand by your honor
yet,for we know were well dealt by before we landed.
Sir Your honor remembers what was concluded upon at
Halifax that we should assist you in public matters and
we are willing to take the trouble off your honors hands
by taking of small matters upon ourselves –
This from your ffriends and well wishers in sincerity
The Sierra Leone Company known by the name of
Beverhout[2]

8. Andrew Moor, 24 August 1792

To The Right Honourable John Clarkeson Esq Captan
Generall and Commander in Chief In and Over the Free
Colony of Searra Leone and Its Dependancys and Vice –
Admaral of the Same etc etc[1]

Whareas your Honours Memorilist Andrew Moors[2]
Wife being brought to bed this morning and Delivered
of a Daughter and now Stands in need of Some
Nourishment for her and the Child your Excellancys
Memorialest begeth that out your Humanity and
Geantle Goodness you Will take it Int your honours
Considaration to Give Orders that She and the Child
have some Nourishmen Such as Oat meal Molassis or
Shugger a Little Wine and Spirits and Some Nut mig and
your Memorialest as in Dutey bound Shall Ever Pray
NB and one[lb] Candles for Light

9. Rose Morral, 5 November 1792

November 5th 1792
Mr Clarkson Sir if it please to Grant Rose morry her
request She have no peace with her husband Sir if it
please your eccellent honnah as to part us or bound him

over to the peace Before your honnah go home to
London in so doing your honnah will oblig your humble
Servent Rose morral

10. Luke Jordan, 18 November 1792

Free Town november 18 1792
To our most eccellent govenor John Clarkson sir if it
please your eccellent honnah as to Consider your
eccellent promise is to mak all man hapy sir we wont to
know wither we is to pay as much for the half rassion as
for the full please your eccellent your eccellent promise
sir the request of the Company please your eccellent
honnah our most eccellency governnor John Clarkson
the people wating for an answer as soon as possible
please your honnah sir ————
the people is willing to give one Days work in a week for
their Rassions
the Captin of the Company Luke Jurdin[1] Captin of the
Bother if it your eccellent honnah to let the Captin know
what your mean to Do

11. John Cuthbert, 19 November 1792

Freetown November 19 1792
To his most Excellency Governor Clarkson that we
would be Glad to See your Excellency Governor on
Shore if your honour pleas and if your honour pleas to
point a place for to met your honour

      John Cuthbert[1]

12. Petition (John Duncome and others),
   19 November 1792

Free Town November 19th 1792
To His Excellency John Clarkson Esq[r]
Sir we would wish by this Oppertunity to inform you
that we are Ready in anything that his in our power for
the preservation of this Colony we lay down our case
open before you which If you pleases to peruse it we
hope you'll take in Consideration that we are under a
very presd situation in the first place we labours hard
with very small wages – which is very loo for the
Expence of tools runs hard as we are Oblidge to have a
good many therefore we are Come to a Rasalition to lay
it before you in hopes yr honour will take in
Consideration towards us we dont wish to offend, we
Could wish as we only works for three shillings p[r] day
to have our provision free or else have our wages raisd
and pay for it by free grace we wish to have our full
provision as work men ought to have and our wages to
be half in hard Cash and the other part in the Coloney
mony[1] by which there will be no grumbling – there is
one thing more that is our allowance in liq[r] in our time of
working for the Climate has a very Requisite Call for it

Witness our hands –

John Duncome	Steven Peters	John Johnson
Cato Perkins	Abram Smith	Daniel Prophet
Thomas Baccas	Thos Quiper	Robert Morris
Peter Frances	Luke Dixon	Phillip Lawrance
Isaac Anderson	Thos Jackson	Anthony Steven
Cato Burden	Wm Furguson	Dem Sillavan
Boston King	John Townsen	Henry Cook
Thos Hogg	Miles Dixon	John Cooper
Summerset Loghan	Richard Webb	
Cesir Smith	Joseph Williams	

Sighn by the above names Munday November 19[th][2]

13. Antson Zizer, 26 November 1792

Freetown November 26   Antson Zizer Capt[1]

To his Excellency Governor John Clarkson
Sir we have taking this opportunety to aquint your
honour Concerning your honour promises that your
honour made to us about the half raison that we was to
give the Company one Day in the week for our half
raision But Now Mr Peppy Said that your honour did
not tell him of it and he is not gone to write his Book for
it and there is Jonas Bracy and Shaddrack Gusses there
thier raison is Stop now if our Excellents Governor will
Consider thee two men thee are willing to Continue in
the Same in the working party therefor your honour will
thank of the wood party
O Sir how Shall we a Dress your honour for what your
honour has under go for us therefor we give your
honour hearty thanks for our Excellent Governor
Goodness may the God of heaven prosper your honour
in all thing that you lad your hand on for we Earthy
worm Can make your honour any reward But the God
of heaven is able Sir to yr honour we would be glad to
get a answer from your Excellency for all my people is
go out to work and the Do Expect to have answer when
they Come out of the wood
No More at present from your Servant Antson Zizer
Capt of the wood party
for we honour your as our father

14. Farewell Petition, 28 November 1792

Sierraleon Freetown November the 28 1792
we the humble pittioners we the Black pepol that Came
from novascotia to this place under our agent John
Clarkson and from the time he met with us in novascotia
he ever did behave to us as a gentilmon in everey rescpt
he provided every thing for our parshige as wors in his

pour to make us comfortable till we arrived at Sierraleon
and his behaveor heath benge with such a regard to to us
his advice his Concil his patience his love in general to us
all both men and wemen and Children and thearfour to
the gentilmon of the Sierloen Companey in England we
thy humbel pittioners wold desier to render thanks to
the honerabl gentilmon of the Sierraleon Companey that
it heth pleased allmighty god to put it into the hearts to
think of them on us when we war in destress and we
wold wish that it might please the gentilmon of the
Companey as our govener is a goin to take his leave of us
and a goin to England thearfour we wold Bee under stud
by the gentilmon that our ardent desier is that the Same
John Clarkeson Shold returen Back to bee our goverener
our had Comander in Chef for the time to com and we
will obay him as our governer and will hold to the laws
of England as far as lys in our pour and as for his promis
to us in giting our lands it is the peopel agree to take
parte of thear land now at present and the remander as
soon as posable and we pray that his Excelency John
Clarkson might Be preserved safe over the sea to his
frinds and return to us again and we thy humbel
pittioners is in duty Bound and will ever pray
witness our hands to the sine

David George	Samson Heywood
Richard Corankeapon	Stephen Ficklin
Catrin Bartley	William Taylor
wider	John Cutworth
Lucy Whiteford	Charity Macgriger
wider	a widow
John Frinken	Henry Lawrance
Boston King	Cato Burdan
Thomas London	John Kizzell
Francis Worak	Ely Ackim
Jacob Smith	Kasscey Cranpone
Francis Partrick	Lazarus Jones
Capt Stpen Peters	John Manuell

Benjamin Francis
his mark
Jess George
John Johnson
Charles Jones
George Weeks
Joseph Williams
Hector Peters
Jane Richard
Elizabeth Wite
Cato Linas
Joseph Ramsey
John Demps
Jacb Wigfall

Georg Williams
Jane Humans wider
Philish Halsted wider
Janey Marshel
Isaac Streeter
John Bevis his mark
John Gray his Brick Layer
Robert Robertson his
Josep Lonard his mark
Thomas Godfrey his mark
Thomas Sandas
Pheby Linch
Georg Black

15. Beverhout Company, 11 December 1792

Thursday December 11th 1792   Free Town

To the Honourable Mr Clarkson Governor of Sirealeone

Most worthy

Sir we the Children of faith do gather our Selves to gether in one body to lay this address before you hoping you will take it in Consideration. we the Children of St John New brumswick do here lay our distress before you Concerning Mr Bebrote he is a man of a worthy Concern but by false hearted trator would wish to do him unjustice pulling down his Bright before god in opposion against him which Causes great Concern to all of his Dear and Sinceir Children of faith – we only here beg his Right he is a true man and a just man in all that ever we see in him so as to be honest sober and Religus in all his dealings we therefore beg that he will not be nomore by y^r Consent in helping him be any more Assulted by those whom would wish so to do him any Injury – we could wish that he could have

the satisfaction of gaining his Place again as assured he is
worthy of it – – we have seen such bad usage showed to
him since their last treatment that grievs our heart by the
usage of others after his attempting to go to the place of
worship to give some Satisfaction to his Children were
mocked and ill behaviour shewn him by thoes that have
no reason so to do – in during his whole time in St John
if he was Called for at any time at night he was always
ready and willing to help a friend By gods Blessing –

from Sir your humble Servant all
Mr Bebrote Company

16. Richard Corankeapoan, 13 June 1793

Sierra leon [June] the 13 1793

honered Sir I take this oppertunety to wright to your
honer to let you know that I am well and I hope that this
Lines may find your honer well and your good Ladey
Sir I am verey glad to hear from your honer and to hear
that you got safe home and to hear of your good suckces
in your marain I gave your Joy honer Joy and god Bless
you and gave you Long Life and may you Both Live
hapey for ever   Sir we are the most of us is verey harty
thear is not maney sick a mong us we have the most of us
drowd our town Lots and are a Building our houses the
pepol is much desatfied with the goods and the
proveisons have got to such a price it is verey dear sence
your honer have Left us Sir Capt deboise[1] is left us four
days ago
thear is some of our pepol will not Be Contented with
aney thing som [indecipherable] but we donot mind
what everey one says But the Body of the Colleney is
Bent for your honer to Com and Be our govener thear is
two men a goin to England to see the Companey with
som papers Isaac Anderson and Cato purkins and to

return a gain as soon as thea have ansur   Sir Rember me
to Davèd [sic] georg[2] his wife is well and all the famley
John Cutbuth[3] and his fameley and I Remain you ever
duteyfull Servent
Richard Corankeapoan[4]

17. Miles Dixon, 14 October 1793

Honoured

    Sir I take this oppertunity of writeing to you to
inform you that I & my family is all well & Remembers
ther love to you & am very happy to hear that you have
arrived safe to London & Gives you great joy in your
undertakings we shoud. be very glad to see you here
again & we hope your honor will take it on yourself to
come & see us once more – My Brothers & Sisters are
well & desires to be remembered to you. The people
would be very glad to see you again as we have not
found things in the same way as you told us when your
honour went away & we have not had any satisfaction
from Mr George of the Companys good will towards us,
& Mr George has spoke very much against you since he
come back from London[1] – Honoured sir I am sorry to
trouble you but goods is scare in the Colony that I will
be oblige to you to send me a bolt of Linning & 3 Good
Hatts if you do not come your self & send me the price
of them & I will pay the money to any of the Gentlemen
in the Colony that your honour may think fit to say – I
have to inform you that the Gospell is begining to
flourish in the Land I hope the Lord will be with you &
yours & I hope the Lord will prosper you in all your
undertakings –

               I am Sir yours
               Miles Dixon[2]
               Free Town 14th Octr 1793
Sir I beg you will send me a Letter in closed with yours
to Mr Putman Esqr in Hallifax Novascotia

18. Cato Perkins and Isaac Anderson, 26 October 1793

London Octr 26.th 1793

Sir

We are very sorry indeed that we have not had the happiness to see you since we came to this Country as we expected to find a great friend in you and was in hopes we should have got you to go out to Sierra Leone again for we assure you Sir all the people there have been much put upon since you came away and we wanted you to go out that you might see justice done us as we had no one besides to look to but you but we are sorry to tell you that the Gentlemen you left behind you speaks mightily against you and we was present when Mr Pepys told all the people that you had no authority for the Promises you made us in Nova Scotia but that you did it of your own accord and that the Company could not perform what you had promised and this bred a great disturbance in the Colony and the people send us home to know from the directors here what they had to depend upon but the Gentlemen have not used us well, and we are sorry for it as we are there things will not go well in the Colony unless the people you brought with you from nova Scotia have justice done them, we did not know where to write to you till Mr Duboz[1] let us and as he is going down we send it by him and we would be very glad to hear from you I have some advice from you we would have been there before now but our expenses would not bear it there If it suits you to Come down we should be very happy to se you, we have heard that your Lady is ill we are sorry for it,

And we are Sir your humble and Faithful Servts
Cato Perkins &
Isaac Anderson[2]

19. Settlers' Petition

To the Hble the Chairman & Court of Directors of the Sierra Leone Company London

The Petition and Representation of the Settlers at
the New Colony of Sierra Leone most humbly sheweth
That your Petitioners the Black Settlers of this Place beg
leave to assure your Honours that they are sincerely
thankful for the good they know your Honrs wished to
do by bringing them from Nova Scotia to this Country
& that they in their hearts admire the wonderful blessing
you wish to spread by Settling this Place – And we wish
to assure your Honrs that there is nothing in our Power
that we would not be very glad to do to help your Honrs
good intentions   But we are much grieved to see your
Honrs and yourselves so much imposed upon and tho
we have bore our hardships a long time now without
groaning but very little We at last feel ourselves so
oppressed that we are forced to trouble your Honrs that
your Eyes as well as ours may be open   The hopes of
helping your Honrs schemes of enjoying the Priviledges
of Freemen of Reaping the benefits accruing from
Religion Industry and Virtue and with the help of God
and your kindness to receive Temporal advantages better
than those we had in Nova Scotia induced us to leave
that Country and come here   The Promises made us by
your Agents in Nova Scotia were very good and far
better than we ever had before from White People and
no man can help saying But Mr Clarkson behaved as
kind and tender to us as if he was our Father and he did
so many humane tender acts of goodness that we can
never forget them and notwithstanding we have suffered
a great many hardships before he left this Country yet we
were willing to look over every thing rather than trouble
your Honours in hopes before this Rainy Season came
on we would have our Land and be able to make a Crop
to support us next year But in Place of that the Rains is
now set in and the Lands is not all given out yet so we
have no time to clear any for this year to come. Health
and life may it please your Honrs is very uncertain and
we have not the Education which White Men have yet

we have feeling the same as other Human Beings and
would wish to do every thing we can for to make our
Children free and happy after us but as we feel our selves
much put upon & distressed by your Council here we
are afraid if such conduct continues we shall be unhappy
while we live and our Children may be in bondage after
us But as we all understand your Honrs intentions
towards us to be very good and as we hear that you are
amongst the best People in England living always with
the Fear of God before your Eyes we think we may let
you know how we are put upon and tell all our
Greevances to you in sure hopes that God will incline
your hearts to listen to us & make us Comfortable. In
Nova Scotia we were very poor but at the time we left
that Country we were just getting into a comfortable
way of living and what little we had to send for ourselves
and Families we could carry to a great many Stores and
lay it out as we pleased and get double as much for it in
many things as we can get here   There is no Store here
but the Company's and the extortionate Price we are
obliged to pay for every thing we have out of it keeps us
always behind hand so that we have nothing to lay out
for a Rainy Day or for our Children after us and we are
sorry to tell your Honrs that tho Mr Clarkson promised
us in Nova Scotia that we should not pay more than Ten
Pounds advance on every Hundred that we are charged
from 50 to 100 pr Cent on almost every thing we buy
since Mr Clarkson went from this Place and we know of
a very bad dishonest action which was done by Mr
Dawe's order which was to put Thirty Gals of Water
into a Pun^n of Rum not one Punch^n but several & then
sell it to us for a Shilling a Gall^n more than we had ever
paid before And please your Honrs we have no Place to
Work but in the Company's Works and we are just at the
mercy of the People you send here to give us what
Wages they Please & charge us what they like for their
Goods and tho we know your Honr wishes us to be

happy but we are sorry to tell you we are just the
reverse. There is please your Honrs People punished
here without a Cause they are turned out of the Service
& afterwards not sufferd to buy any Provisions from the
Store & where else can they buy any thing for all the
Money we have is Paper Money or such other Money as
will not pass any where else and Mr Dawe's who is the
Governor at present shows so much partiality to some
People & so much dislike to others and he does so many
things which seems to us to be very much out of the
Character of a Governor that we do not think your
Colony will ever be settled unless you out some Person
besides and Mr Dawes seems to wish to rule us just as
bad as if we were all Slaves which we cannot bear but we
do not wish to make any disturbance in the Colony but
would chuse that every thing should go on quietly till we
hear from you as we are sure we will then have justice
shown us for we have a great deal of Confidence in you
and we have never known since we came here what
footing we are on but are afraid concerning the
happiness of our Children for as we have not Justice
shewn us we do not expect our Children after us will
unless your Honrs will look into the matter

    When Governor Clarkson left us he told us that Mr
Pepys would give us all our Lots of Land in two Weeks
after he went away and he called upon us all and took
leave of us and told us that was to be the case and we
were contented tho we were to get but one Fifth part of
what we were promised but that we were willing to look
over knowing that your Honrs were imposed upon
about the Land here and as we made ourselves certain
that your Honrs would make up all that to us by and by
but we are afraid these things are not told to your Honrs
as they are here and we are doubtful about our Fate and
the Fate of our Children as the Promises made us has not
been perform'd and some of the White Gentlemen here
has told us that all Mr Clarkson promised us he had no

authority for doing & we wish to know if that is the case
for we do not believe it as we have a great opinion of Mr
Clarkson and do not think he would say any thing he
had not authority for and if your Honours would give us
leave to chuse a Governor for our selves we would chuse
Mr Clarkson for he knows us better than any Gentleman
& he would see every thing he Promised us Performed as
so clear up his own Character for when the Gentlemen
you send here talks one against another and does not
agree among themselves we cannot think things are
going on right and we wish your Honrs to know all
these things and we wish your Honrs to know that we
might have had our Lands long ago if Mr Pepys had
done as he ought to do and if there had been no White
Man here we could have laid out the Lots our selves for
many of us have been used to Surveying and we could
have laid out all the Lots in Two Months in place of that
Mr Pepys has been Ten Months and not done them yet
and we are afraid they have cost your Honrs a great deal
of Money but Mr Pepys might have had them done
according to his Promise to Mr Clarkson but he took off
the People that was working on them to build a Fort
which please your Honrs we do not think will ever be
done but will cost your Honrs a great deal of Money and
we think it is a great pity that your Money should be
thrown away but Mr Dawes says he would not mind to
lose One Thousand Pound of your Honours money
rather than not do what he wishes and this expression
was made by Mr Dawes because we complaind that our
wages was low and the Goods was high & he refused to
raise our Wages but put a higher price on the Goods and
we are sorry to tell your Honours that we feel ourselves
so distressed because we are not treated as Freemen that
we do not know what to do and nothing but the fear of
God makes us support it until we know from your
Honrs what footing we are upon and please your Honrs
we wish you to know that the Land Mr Pepys has laid

out for us is in most Places so very bad and Rocky that
we never can make a living on it and we wish your
Honrs could take all these things into Consideration for
we would not trouble you if we had not very good cause
and the Minds of every body here is so distressed about
their situation & about the fate of their Children that we
have chosen Mr Isaac Anderson and Mr Cato Perkins
who is a Preacher of the Gospel to take this Petition to
England and lay our distressed Case before your Honrs
they are both very good Men and whatever your Honrs
agree upon with them we will be satisfied with And if
your Honours will take compassion on us and look into
our Case and see us done Justice by we will always pray
to God to bless you and everything belonging to you
and we will let our Children know the good you do us
that they may Pray for you after it please God to call our
Souls and we the following Hundreds and Tythings and
Preachers of the Gospel do sign this Petition in behalf of
all the Settlers in this Place[1]

20. Cato Perkins and Isaac Anderson, 30 October 1793

Mr John Clarkson   London Octr 30 1793
                                                      No 13 Finch Lane
Hon^d. Sir

     We send you the Petition which we brought from
our Fellow Settlers at Free Town and we hope you will
not see any thing in it that is not true for we declare Sir
we want nothing but what you Promised us and we look
upon you so much our Friend that we think you will see
us done Justice by

Lady Ann Huntingdon[1] has put Mr Perkins to Colledge
till he leaves this Country   We are
        Sir your Faithful Humble Servants
            Cato Perkins
            Isaac Anderson

21. Isaac Anderson and Cato Perkins, 9 November 1793

London Novr.9th 1793

hon^d. Sir

We are much obliged to you for the answer you sent to our Petition and we want to see you very much for we understand that the Company intend to send us out in the Amy and they will not give us any answer but send us back like Fools and we are certain Sir that if they serve us so that the Company will lose their Colony as nothing kept the People quiet but the thoughts that when the Company heard their Grievances they would see Justice done them – and we should be sorry any thing bad should happen but we are afraid if the Company does not see Justice done to us they will not have Justice done to them so we want to see you very much as we think you wish us so well that you could keep us from being wronged if you can

We are Hon^d. Sir
Your Obedt Serts
Isaac Anderson
Cato Perkins

No 13 Finch Lane

22. Isaac Anderson, 11 February 1794

London febry:11:94

Honrd

Sir I tacke this opertunety to Inform you I have Recd several Letters from the peopel of Sira Lone In all of them the have desired me to Let you know how much the are Consarned to know wane the shall ever have the plesuer of seen you and your Good Lady aney moor at Sira Lone if the Cane have a hope of it it will Be much joy to them the all Joines is Senceer Good will and humbel Respects for you Both wishing you may Jnoy Every Blessen in this Life and hapenes in the next is the

prayr of all the peopel of that place pray Sir Excpe of my
kind Respects to you and Mrs Clarkson hope you are
Both well I have not Been very well for some time But
God have spared me till now in marcy

Your humbel Sarvant
at Command Isac Anderson

PS. Hond Sir I wishe to Inform you that things must
Remain silant till I Recd some answer from the peopel of
Sira Lone wich expect soon the Gentelman of the
Companey have wrote for that porpose I am sorrey to
Inform you that the York is Lost in that harber[1] I know
not how it hapen[d] But shall in a few Days the Lapwing is
safe arived in the River I have not seen aney Letter yet
pleas to direct to me at the Sira Lone House[2] then I shall
Recd it safe

23. Luke Jordan and Isaac Anderson, 28 June 1794

Honoured

Sir, These comes with my sincere love to you in
hopes this may find you & your kind lady in good helth,
I have with much concern to lay before your honour an
accident that has happened on the 20 of June[1] As you
was the person we expected was to settle us but in stead
of being settled our situation is worse than when you left
us – Through the misconduct of our later Governor
Zachary Macaulay we are in great confusion When we
acquainted him that these accidents would happen he
would not pay any attention to us & still he says we are
men appointed as peace officers but does not respect us
as such We have with sorrow to acquaint you that the
times is not as it was when you left us as our present
Governor allows the Slave Traders to come here and
abuse us & the Governor up holds them in it & then if
any of the settlers speaks to them concerning there abuse
the Governor thinks it proper to turn them out of the

Companys employ & on that account it has much stired
up the people in confusion as there was a Captain of a
slave ship upset off this place about the first of Juin &
came in here on his way home & began to threaten some
of the people working at the wharf & saying in what
manner he would use them if he had them in the West
Indies And some of the people told him if he came there
to abuse them they would not allow it & on that account
the Governor thought proper to turn them from the
Company's service & on account of the little satisfaction
we had from the Honourable Sierra Leone Company the
Gentlemen here thinks proper to use us in a very
improper manner & in saying why do we not send two
more men to England we are sorry to think that we left
America to come here to be used in that manner & then
to receive no satisfaction from the Honourable Court of
Directors we should be glad if you could make it
convenient to come and see us once more as we all wait
with a longing desire to see you we are all still where you
left us in the Brothers Street[2] & we have lost none that
you left except a few young children born since you left
us we are sir your sincere friend & Hum[ble]

Servt Luke Jordan[3]
Isaac Anderson

Freetown June 28th 1794

24. Luke Jordan and others, 19 November 1794

Sierra Leone Nov[r] 19.1794

To John Clarkson Esq[r]
A Most Respectable Friend to Us the Settlers in Sierra
Leone ——— In Your Being here we wance did call it
Free Town but since your Absence We have A Reason to
call it A Town of Slavery ——— Be not offended of our
Saying so – We take it our duty to write unto to You
letting you know that the French have Attacked us and

Destroy all the Compy Property and likewise our little
Affects.[1] But thanks be God I Raly believed that God see
the tyranny and oppression that are upon us and send
the Message of his Power to attack the Barbarous Task
Masters in the Hight of their Pomp and Oppression and
furthermore after the Enemy have Pity Our Case and
Bestowed A little few Necessary upon us the
Superintended are Desirous to take away from us by
Empression and Signify to say that we have took the
Company Property ———— may it please your honour
Sir – but wonce consider – if any man see Aplace is to be
Destroyed by fire and Run the Risk of his life to care of
that Ruin Afore it is Destroyed do you not think the
Protector of these articles have a just Right to these
property altho the Articles is not of much Consequence
Which is a few Boards and one little Notion A Nother –
but may it please your honour if the Superintended had
the least Consideration to come as Ask Us in a fare
Manner if we will Bestow these things to the Company –
God only knows we would give it up with all Respect –
but in stead of it he came with that Empression to tell us
if we did not give them up we should Never be
Employ'd in the Compy Work nor not any more to be
looked upon but shall be Blotted Out of the Companys
Book – but However we look unto God – furthermore
he never was the man that Ever gav'd us any Amanition
to protect our Selves or Else the French should have
never plundered the Place as they did for we would run
the Risk of saving some of the Companys Property he
had the Enteligence three days afore the French
Attacked Us – and after seeing the Enemy of the Cape he
never would fire nor give us leave but lett the Enemy
come in Broadside of the town and fire upon us then all
hopes was taken Away by firing kild one person and
Wounded two that one dyed the day After and it was the
means of Cutting the Others mans legs – we do Raly
look to see you with ever Longing Eyes – Our Only

Friend – John Clarkston Esqr it Raly will give us
Pleasure to see you Or hear from your Excellancy –
                    Your Well Wishers –

Luke Jordan	Moses Wilkinson preacher
Jn° Jordan	Isaac Anderson
Rubin Simmons	Stephen Peters
America Tolbert	Jas. Hutcherson

A great many More
   the Paper wont afford[2]

25. Sundry Settlers, 16 April 1795

Minutes of Governor and Council 21 April 1795

A letter received from sundry Settlers of which the
following is a <u>literal</u> copy, viz –

Freetown 16th April 1795
To the Honourable Governor & Council of Sierra
Leone
Sirs,
       We take upon ourselves to write unto you by way
of petition begging that we all may become as people
united togather as one – dealing lawfully just & right one
to another – knowing justice are the works of God – &
lett us with godly freedom mantain that which is just
doing no injury. We are the people of the Mathodist
connection that are calld people of a ranglesome nature
wish not to be under the compelment of law & it is so
mention to the Sierra Leone company that we are a
ranglesome sett of people in the Colony, but may it
please your Honours Gentlemans of the Council we are
a sett of People wish not to rule with envy or
empression, but are willing to be under the complement
of any proposhall that is just. Furthermore sir honoured
Gentlemens we are about to mention to you the reason
why we never sign any of the contraction that ever was
proposed by Mr Macaulay.

1st, Your honours very well knows that we had a law,
but God has ordained it so that the Enmy has Atakd us
2nd, & by doing that we all are or was become prisoners
untill we was relieved either by the Company's ships, or
by His Majesty shippings to protect us from our
Emprisenment before we can astablish any laws 3rd,
thay was a great many proposhalls propose by Mr
McCawly which we thought was not proper to Establish
ourselves to any law except what was raly contracted by
the Company, but however we was desirous to content
ourselves living in peace and quitness & to rest all
proposhall untile we can further heare from the
Company whether it was there determination to carry
on the Settlement of the Colony or no – which if it was
there desire we was willing to come under the
Complement of their Laws knowing that they was
Gentlemans of that character that would not wish not to
contract any unjust laws but that witch to maintain truth
& freedom & by our doing so we are counted
mischiefmakers in the Colony. Which may it please your
honours to lett you all know that we are for peice &
quietness, we will propose to you if it is your honours
good pleasure to look into the Circumstance we will
take it upon ourselves to chuse out a few Mens to be our
tideings which we would further here the intention of
the Company & whatever thay would wish to do, & we
make no doubt Gentlemans that thay have been a great
many complaints brought in against us that we was not
desarving of which we humbly beg that if any person or
persons will carry the toung of Atail Bearer against any
of his fellow Creatures to bring them & there Enformers
face & face then we shall have some Regulation in the
Colony, if not we do not think nor expect we will come
upon any determination regulation afore we have that
done – & may it please your honours Gentlemans the
reason why we do this thay are many persons of a very
hasty temper knowing not how to discourse to their

superiors officers which these Mens we ordain to lay in all of our complaints – that the Governor & Council not to be interrupted by every person – which be thay names Nathanl. Snowball[1] Luke Jordan & Jonathan Glasgow[2] which if it is your honours will that we should mention our names, we will also do it, which we will be desirous of an answer

We are Gentlemans
Your humble Servants

26. Settlers, 22 April 1795

Minutes of Governor and Council 28 April 1795

Free Town April 22 1795

To the Honourable Governor & Counsil of Sierra Leone

Sirs. we once more take the liberty of writting to the Governor & Counsil –

we have received the answer of the letter sent to your honours but by receiving it we are oblidge further to answer it – we have most humbly took upon ourselves to make our application to your honours but you have sent to us about Deliviring up the Companys property – which we would be glad further to know if the Governor and Counsil ever did give any of us the Companys property in our persesion that thay should be A Enquery about any such things as farr as our Recoliction we do not recolict that we ever had any property of the Companys in our persesion – if we have there is no Objection – when the French took the place – what property of theirs that thay had no use for – they gave us the priviledge of takeing which we run a great risk in taking – and we raly do not think it is the Companys Entention to ever take one single mite of what we had from the French and furthermore we do not think the Company is the loosers of what property was taken – for we raly think that we are the Distressors

– for whatever property the French took from us – we
have now found the loss which may it please your
honours Gentlemans if the Governor or his Counsil
wanted to have any Clames upon the people for any
property thay should not so quick surrender to the
Enemy – for there was people ready to protect the
Colony – but it was objected and said it was better not to
Resent – however if the Governor and his Counsilars
have gave us the liberty of secureing what we could for
Entention of the Company – we would take it as a great
pleasure Because all thuse privileges was Related to
Government but he would not Embrace those offers
which if thay had we make no objection but it should
been Return but however knowing thay distrissed the
place we supplyd Government with Good many
Nesesary's that we thought would accomode him throw
our own kindness which we was not under any
obligation to do – not only after all of our kind offices
we have done we find there is no kindness showd but we
are further empresed upon which we look upon it to be a
great deal of Emposision which we do not think ever to
come upon any such terms – for if we do we look upon
ourselves to be the greater fools for so doing for we have
long ago been Empresed upon with Tyranny and
Emprision which we are determined not any longer to
be so but to Enjoy the privileges of Freedom – which if
our Request can not be complyd by government as we
would not wish to make any strife – we will lay all of our
greviances to the Court of Directors if not Parlament
must act its part – for we yet do not know upon what
footing we are upon wheather to be made Slaves or to
only go by the name of Freedom

        which we still remain your humble servants
                         Settlers

We will be glad of an answer

27. John Cooper, 14 January 1796

Sierra Leone January 14th 1796

Most Worthy Sir

This is from me your well wisher and fellow Sufferer – it
was my Entention long ago to pay my Address to you
knowing that it was my duty so to do. but by
Disappointments and Difficulties I was Oblidge further
to detain it. but most Worthy and most honoured Sir as
much as I know that it is my duty by this opportunity I
have now Endeavoured and hopeing that I may be of no
Offence. but by this my Undertaking that it may be a
more Sattisfaction on my Side – altho the Promises that
you Undertook by Authority and was Disappointed we
know that the fault laid to the S.Leone Company – but it
is by A Contsenteous feeling that I know that if it was In
your power – that it would long ago been fulfilled. but
most Esteemed Sir let that be Not your Grief – it is our
Ernest Desire that you was Amongst us for we are here
Used with tyranny and Oppression. but we are
Confidence that your feeling for us lays at our Own
breast.

I am Sir and as in duty bound I shall ever pray – I will
be glad to be remembered to your good lady –

I am Sir and What is more to your honour your most
humble & Obdt St Jn°. Cooper, Carpenter S.Leone[1]

28. James Liaster, 30 March 1796

Free Town Sierra Leone March 30 1796

To

the honourable Jn°. Clarkson

honoured Sir this is from me your humble Servant and
fellow Sufferer

Oh may it please your honour that you ever leaved this
Colony. for the day that you leaved it we was very much
Oppress by Goverment and many that did not wish
your honour well wish that you was at this time here. for

many of us is sorely repented that we ever Came to this place but by a feeling that your honour would be here with us made many of us. We Believe that it was the handy work of Almighty God – that you should be our leader as Mosis and Joshua was bringing the Children of Esaral to the promise land – kind Sir and honoured Sir be not Angry with us all but Oh that God would Once more Give you A Desire to come & visit us here. which we expect if it was not the Goodness of God to give us Our Mother wit we would be all Slaves. but Blessed be unto his holy Name they have took all of my property land and house Only On Suspetion that I had some Goods when they gave up the Colony to the French in A most Scandolas Manner which if we Even had Arms they mought took the place but Never landed but theese things was kept back and by Seeing Our Selfe so much Oppress we have Got A Considarable Quantity of land at Pirots bay from prince George[1] and a Grant giving unto us by the heads for ever which we are now Cutting down the Town ready to move Next dry – Which we have Oppointed Mr Snowball Jurdan & Glasgow heads of Settlement Which you will your selfe here further About it from them by the Jane Vessel. Which if you think it is better send us Word.

and hopeing my letter will find you and your Good lady well and all All of your Relations beging to be remembered to them

And so no more from me But God Bless you & all your Good family

I am Sir & what is more to your honour

Your most Obt humble Servt   James Liaster[2]

Farewell

God Bless you

God Bless you

and prosper you that you may have

A Crown in Heaven laid up for you

29. James Hutcherson and Moses Murray, 24 May 1796

Free Town S.Leone May 24 1796

Dear

and most kind Sir –

I wance more take this Conveniant Opportunity of Writting to you and your Good family hopeing threw the tender Mercies God to find them well and by knowing it is my bound and Duty to lett you know the Situation of this place since your Absence – but Oh the Great Grief We received it is mostly unknown to make Mention – but our Oppressions is very great for ido raly Believe that thay was many that did not Wish you well. but they have Raly now found it to their Great Greaf – you have several times laid down before us the Oppression that King Pharoh Where With Oppressed the Egyptians – seaveral of us have laid that saying in our hearts we know find our Selves truly Oppress – but Oh kind sir and good sir. I think that I can spend Number of days in Ading my Recolections to this letter but the opportunity is so Express I am Oblidge to Conclude. but Honoured Sir leave us Not in the Wilderness to the Oppressing Masters – but be Amongst us.

As you have took that Great undertaking As Mosis & Joshua did – be with us Until the End

And so No more but God Bless you and your Good family and Give you A Desire to Visit us

> I am kind Sir
> I am good Sir
> and What is More to your
> [obliterated]
> your most humble & Obedient
> Servt
>> James Hutcherson[1]
>> Mosis Murry[2]

30. Nathaniel Snowball and James Hutcherson, 24 May 1796

Free Town Sierra Leone May 24 1796

Most

kind sir – knowing it is my duty I have by this Conveniant Opportunity endeavour to write to your Most Worthy honour hopeing to find you and your good family well. but not as it leaves me. for why by reason of the Oppression Wherewith we are Oppress. but I am Chosin out the head of A Number of people to take my Departure as the Ezerlites did. When we may be no longer in bondage to this tyranious Crew. for I look upon it good to lay our Grieviances to your honour. Altho I make No Doubt but there is many that would wish not to promote your happyness but they With Sorrow lament. but as you have forsake us it is my Determination to take my Jurney from this Colony to Pirots Bay at the Next Dry as we already have the town Cut Down being a piece of ground freely Given to us with A grant from Prince George Jemmy Queen and the heads About. and my friendly Well Wisher if it is in your power to promote Our happiness there we look on your Worthy honour – I would have send the Names and Number of the people but by the Expressness of the Dispatch of the Vessel I am Oblidge to rest it until A Nother Opportunity but I make no Doubt but these people is your Well Wishers

I have wrote seaveral letters Afore but Never heard Wheather you had receive them or No.

So No more from me at this Opportunity

But kind Sir and good Sir What is more to your honour

I am good Sir your humble and Obediant Sarvant

Nathaniel Snowball

James Hutcherson

all the people in my Town begs to be kindly remembered to you and your good family –

31. ␣niel Snowball, 29 July 1796

␣96

ir

We are persuaded from that
␣e already discovered towards us
␣ hear we & the Colony people at
␣ & spirits.

w␣ ␣ t such an union as is very
desireable ␣␣ p␣␣ in our situation does not exist
among us. There are as there always have been divisions
among us; indeed Mr George & some of his people seem
to think they can do no greater service for the Company
or Colony than to invent & carry all the lies in their
Power to the Governor against those who differ from
them in things which pertain to religion.
The land which we understand you gave us we have had
difficulty to hold in our possession.
There have been two tryals concerning it & in the last
the jury gave it in our favour but as yet the matter is not
quite settled.[1]
We could say many things but after all it will amount to
no more than this that we love you, and remember your
Labours of love & compassion towards us with
Gratitude, & pray that Heaven may always smile on you
& yours. We have the honor & happiness to be, Sir your

Most obedient & humble servants

Luke Jordan
Nathaniel Snowball

Daddy Moses[2] wishes his love to you

32. Boston King, 1 June 1797

Hon^d & very Dear Sir

I gladly address you with thes few lines hoping they will find you & Mrs in good health which blessing at presint I enjoy thanks be to God Dear Sir I promous you to inform you of the state of the Colony at all time I now think it my Duty to state it in the folowing manner – there is about six or nine Family leave the Colony and gon down to Cuckel bay¹ & more is about to go Snow Bawl & Family Peter Weak & his Family York Ranson And Family Dick Lawrance & his Sabbage & his Jhon Cupper & his Cupper again & his Primous Oggden & his Family Samual Gullet And his Family Cesar Brat & his And many other Familys is thinking of going when the Rin id over & it appire that their cheif reason is because the Company enQuire quit rent for their Lands a yea ago but the people will not compy with it I should not wonder if one half of the Colony should [undecipherable] one thing Dear Sir I can say that the Colony is In Peace at preasent & Grate nuber is gon is out on their Farme and their are biden fair for som of them is liveing endepence who naims will be to Tegus to mension. Hon^d Sir I will take it as a grate favour if you will me a Quire of Paper for the Paper they sell is not fit to rite on I bage lso for a few pends. I shall try to Send Mrs Clarkson some nuts when I can find Convaance

I remin Your sincere
Friend Boston King²
June the 1 1797 Sierra Leone
Free Town Africa

PS Give my kind Love to Mr Witbread

33. Boston King, 16 January 1798

Hon^d Sir

It this indeed out of my power To express to
you the regard most of your People Still bear toward
your Hon^d the Natise as well as us all even those at
Baullum shore; I thanks you for your Friendly advise
you Give me in your letter I receive the 12 of Dec & For
you satterfaction I have precur you one of the Governor
Pmphle in which you will find the Movening cause of all
The disturbance in the place & This is som of the reason
why so many Family leave the Colony & I blieve if I did
nont speake So much to them of what you say to me
whil I was with you in England I raly think they would
be more family leave the Colony But I am thankfull for
it that at presst our Colony is in peace, and the last year
The greatest parts of the people mad such a noble crop
that I may say with The greates propriety that if the
Lord will give ous suckcess this yeare I have now Doubt
but the gratter parts of the people may Become
Independence.
Mr Anderson Moses Wilkerson & Stven Peters join me
to you
And all of your People as many as I was dare to show
your letter to and the Cry of all is O! that God would
fabour them one mor with your pressent. the Hat I have
gave to Mr Domingo¹ & he turn you many thanks for it
& Gave his sarvast to you & Mrs Clarkson. Dear Sir I
think of sining one small box of fly to Mr Withbread² if
you think it will be excepable to him & one bottle of
sandepey. Much more Might be said but time will not
admit of it And Belief Sir Should be glad to heir from
you at all times when it this convenence. do you know
Dear Sir that Mr Thornton³ after promous me my passag
if I wantd work And only because I came don the river
to see you that time He desired Cappin Smith to charge
15 Ginny but Sir I regardeth not because I know I shall
able to Pay them and I do ashoure it will only serve To

attach my love more to you because I know it was only
out of spite.

PS Give my Lov to Mrs Clarkson   I remaine your
                                   affectionate
                                   Friend Boston King
                                   January the 16 1798

34. Isaac Anderson, 21 January 1798

Hon[d] Sir

              this come with my best Repect to you
hopping they will find you and Your in good health as
these leave me at Pressent and Mt family. I have sent
Your Hon[d] a small Barrl of Rice Of my own produce,
which I hope your Hon[d] will Except of for it is said
Thou shall not mushel the ox that Treadet out the Corn[1]
& If so how much More is Your Hon[d] ought to be
Estened More them an ox hond have sheaw the same
affection with ous all in this Place as well as in Amarica
then for in all thing it is Rasonable that the Husbanman
ought first to Pertak of the Fruth. the friends joine with
me to you & Mr King Have sent you a letter with a
Phemplet[2] by Peter Corner[3]

              I am Dear Sir your Affectionate Friend
                     Isaiah Anderson
                     January the 21 1798
                        Sierra Leone
                        Africa

35. Isaac Streeter and George Carrol, 5 August 1797

Minutes of Governor and Council 17 August 1797

Received and read a Letter from the Hundredors and
Tythingmen of which the following is a copy –

Sir   August 5th 1797

   we are to inform you that we have left Lands to come

here in expectation to receive Lands in the same
condition as we received them in Nova Scotia. But we
find it to the Contrary of that, for we find that the
Company says the Land is theirs. Sir if we had been told
that, we never could come here on that condition, for
before we will pay the shilling per acre we will reply to
Government for lands or to the Kings of the Country.
Sir we are astonished why the Company could not tell us
after three years we was to pay a shilling per acre. Sir we
are Deceived by some misunderstanding for the
Company says that the Land is belonging to them and if
it is theirs, there is the Lands they may take it if they
think proper in so doing. Sir this dispute is on account of
the Rents for if the Lands is not ours without paying a
shilling per acre, the Lands will never be ours, no not at
all, and if we are Ignorant of the Matter we wish that the
Governor would show to us as we may show to the
people.

This matter is approved of by the hundredors
Sir Please your honour we will be happy of an
answer as we may give answer to the people
Signed by Isaac Streeter Chairman of the Tything
George Carrol Chairman of the
Hundredors[1]

36. Ishmael York, Stephen Peters and Isaac Anderson, 16 January 1798

Minutes of Governor and Council 16 January 1798

The letter is <u>literally</u> as follows –

To the Honorable Captn Ball Esqr
Commander of his majestys Ship the Dudless

Honour Sir

We the hundreors & tything of this place having find
ourselves opresed would wish to address your honour
with these few lines to lay frefore your honour all our

grievances and our distresses which we are incontring
with here. First we received a Proclamation from
government for our good behaviour in the last war,
which was brought to us by one Mr John Clarkson &
told us that government had heard of our complaints
been in a Cold Country would remove us to Sierra
Leone where we may be comfortable This when we
received it from Mr Clarkson we gladly exsepted of the
offer from his Majesty. And found shiping & Provision
& brought us here. And hoving now find we are
oppressed we would wish to know whether we are shut
out from government or whether we remained his
subject or not which if we are his subject we be glad to
know from your honour if we has not a right to
appleyed to government to see ourselves righted in all
the wrongs which are Done to us here since we been,
Now if your honour will take a view & see how
Dissalute we are, what petty forts you see a long the
water side Done out of our own expence been poor not
able to make the place sufficantly strong to protect us
again we have all the roads to Clean ourselves and all our
poor are upon ourselves and after all this been burden
with our poor roads Bridges & all the burden of the
place we are shamefully Called upon to pay a quit-rent
of a shilling a actr for the land which we hold Sir we are
sorry to informed your honour that we are not used here
as free settlers we humbly begs an answer to this –

> We are Sir
> your honour most humble servts
> Ishmael (mk) York[1] &
> Stephen Peters &
> Isaac H.Anderson

P.S. We shall take it kind if your honour will Called a
meeting to have a hearing between us & the Governor

37. Resolutions of the Hundredors and Tythingmen, August-September 1799

Minutes of Governor and Council 10 September 1799

The following Resolutions of the Hundredors and Tythingmen were laid before the Governor and Council for their concurrence, viz –

August the 31.1799

Resolved that all Persons having lots of lands either in Freetown or Granvl town[1] shall clear one half of the street adjoining their lots before the first of October next, and they shall al so clear the Grass within their lots down by the same time, and all Persons neglecting for to obey this law shall be fine ed in the sum of fifteen shillings, the money to be paid in the hands of how shall be A pointed Surveyor, Miles Dixon pointed, he is for to have one shilling for every lot that he get clair, the maney to be youse by the concent of the Hundreddors and Tythingmen and Governor and Council And for the lands of the Company's is to be cleained by the Governor and charge to the Company.

> Signed by James Robertson[2]
> Chairmon his X mark
> Nathaniel Wansey Dbt Chairmon[3]
> his X mark

John Stephensen A Pointed Surveyor for Granvill Town And he is to have the same as Miles Dixon[4] one shilling for his trouble for every lot

> Proved by the Hundreddors and signed by Thomas Freeman his X mark[5]

Augist 31.1799

At a full meeing of the Tythingmon and com on a Relusution that all for enners coming in the Coleny of Sierra Leone for to live as a Seetlor, they shall pay a sum

of money for the good of the Coloney. And the sum that
they shall pay is to be fixed by hundreddors and
tythingmon and the Governor and Council, and their is
to be a Corlector point by the Hundreddors and
tythingmon, and the money is not to youse ed without
the concent of hundreddors and tythingmon and
Governor and Council

> Signed by James Robertson
> Chairmon his X mark
> Nathaniel Wansey Dbt Chairmon
> his X mark

Proved by the hundreddors and signed by
> Thomas Freeman his X mark

Septr. the 7th.1799

At a full meting of the tythingmon and Com on a
Relusution that the Nova Scotia who com with Mr
Clarkston adjoining the Granville People with them,
they are the Propriatives of the Colenney and No for
enners shall com in as a right of makeing of Lawes with
ought the concent of the Hundreddors and tythingmon.
Nor shall they have a vote with ought their concent.

> Signed by James Robertson
> Chairmon his X mark

Proved by the Hundreddors and signed by
> Thomas Freeman
> his X mark

38. Nathaniel Wansey, 13 February 1800

Minutes of Governor and Council, 4 March 1800

The following list of grievances was presented by the
Hundredors and Tythingmen to the Governor and
Council, vizt. Copy

Feby 13th 1800

Sir

We take an occasion to shew the hurt
according to Mr Ludlam's request. Mr Ludlam's request
was to shew every particulars wherein we were injured.
1. We are willing to shew that we cannot get justice from
the White people. Because the time of the man beating
Mr York & like to have drowned him. Mr York came up
and made a regular complaint to Mr Gray thinking at the
present they they were my superior officers. Mr Ludlam
and Mr Gray both turned against me & plead for the
man at the same time Having sufficient witnesses that I
never opened my mouth to the man & the Man
confessing himself that I never said a word to him. That
is one plain matter to shew that we stand in need of
Judges & Justices. If there was a place of an appeal I
should have recompence fully.
2 I have been much opposed by Mr Macaulay at the time
when I was robed of an 100 and odd Dollars who shall I
go to seek Recompence for a fals accusation[1] That is
another hurt to shew you that we stand in need of Judges
& Justices   3 I have another thing to shew you that we
settlers will take our money and go to the store and we
will be turned away with our paper money that they
make in our hands and Cannot get such things as we
want At the same time the slave traders can come and be
supplied when ever they think proper.   4. Sir We would
not wish to entrude upon the Company's store for any
thing without money no further than the Gentlemen of
the store saw proper. But we would wish to be used
according to the Company's promise beleiving every
thing they said at the time. But for the unjust usage we
now doubts and we hault upon the oppinion. But when
we come to consider the Matter is great that a White man
will always follow a Blackman Because it is for their own
ends they expects gains Because we are ignorant –
5 I have another thing to ask Sir Did you ever know in
Ireland in Scotland or in England that a Gentleman at a

public auction will till another Gentleman that is a
freeholder that he will not take his bid. We have been
used as such at the Company's stores selling of damaged
goods. Thats one point of Unjustice.   6 We would wish
to explain this. We do not think it is proper that a
Company servant should stand up among a parcel of
men and Rebuke them But if they have ought against
any man to mention his name to let him come Forth and
answer for himself and not to harber tail bearing and
News carrying Because Sir where there are such things
Harbered and carried forward there can be no peace in
that place Neither can the place prosper but hard
thoughts and murmurings arises by such traduction and
all these traduction proceed from the Companys
Servents and it is very hard to think that a man will not
take what he makes.

7. Because we perceive that the place grows worse and
worse every day the time of Mr Clarkson and Mr
Dawses present Shiping was not allowed to come here to
shew any authority[2] Neither to caninade the place
raising of a Mutiny and Disturbing of the Native Chief
and the Settlers which is liable to bring on War upon the
Settlers Neither in the time of Mr Clarkson and Mr
Dawes proceeding they did not refuse taking the money
that they made for any thing at all that they had in their
Stores it is so here and carried on in these days and we
think that is a hard pint of unjustice View England
Scotland and Ireland and consider which is your native
Country if they was to deny their own coin how would
they live

I am sorry to see that the white people strives to blind
the eys of the Simple which we have seen them
endeavoured from our youth.

I address you with this I am your most humble Servent

Signed by Nathaniel Wansey Chairmon of the Tything
Mon his X mark

39. Paper of Laws, 3 September 1800

Paper of Laws stuck up at Abram Smith's house by the Hundredors and Tythingmen[1]

Sept 3rd 1800. – If any one shall deny the Settlers of any thing that is to be exposed of in the Colony, and after that shall be found carrying it out of the Colony to sell to any one else, shall be fined £20 or else leave the Colony,and for Palm Oil 1/–[2] Quart,whoso ever is found selling for more than 1/– Quart is fined 20/– Salt Beef 6d.lb. any one selling for more shall pay the fine of 40/– and Salt pork 9d.lb.shall pay the fine of 40/– and for rice 50 cwt. to a Dollar 5/– and whosoever is found selling for less than for a Dollar shall pay the fine of £10 and Rum is to be 5/– Galln.at the wholesale and any one that sells for more than 5/– shall pay the fine of £3 and the Retailer is not to sell for more than 6/3 by the Gallon and to sell as low as a Gill at 6/3 Gallon as low [*sic*] a single glass as 3 Cents and if any one should sell for more than that shall pay the fine of £3 Soap at 15d.lb. and whosoever shall sell for more than 15d. shall pay the fine of 20/–. Salt Butter 15d.lb. and if any more than 15d.lb. shall pay the fine of 20/– and if any one found keeping a bad house is fined 20/– or for abuse £1 for trespass 10/– for stealing shall pay for twice the value for stealing,a blow £5 for removing his neighbour's landmark shall pay £5 for cutting timber or wattles on any person's land without their leave shall pay £5 for drawing a weapon or any edge tool shall pay £5 and for threatening shall pay £2.10 and for lying or scandalizing without proof shall pay £2.10 for Sabbath breaking shall pay the fine of 10/– Cheese to be sold at 1/– lb. and if more than 1/– shall pay the fine of 20/– Sugar 15d.lb.and whosoever is found selling for more than 15d. is fined of 20. And if any man shall serve a summons or warrant or execution without orders from the hundredors and Tythingmen must pay the fine of £20. And if any person shall kill a goat,hog,or sheep or cause her to slink[3] her young shall pay the fine

of £5 or shall kill Cow or Horse shall pay the fine of
£5,and if a man's fence is not lawful he cannot recover
any damage,and if a man that has a wife shall leave her
and go to another woman,shall pay the fine of £10 and if
a woman leave her husband and take up with another
man he shall pay £10,and if Children shall misbehave
they shall pay a fine of 10/– or otherwise be severely
corrected by their parents.

   And this is to give notice by the Hundredors and
Tythingmen that the laws they have made that if the
Settlers shall owe a debt to the Company they shall come
to the Hundredors and Tythingmen and prove their
account,and swear to it and swear to every article
agreeable to the proclamation that they shall take the
produce for their goods and not for their goods pay any
per Cent on it,and all that come from Nova Scotia, shall
be under this law or quit the place. – The Governor and
Council shall not have any thing to do with the Colony
no farther than the Company's affairs,and if any man
shall side with the Governor, etc. against this law shall
pay £20.

   This is to give notice that the law is signed by the
Hundredors and Tythingmen and Chairman they
approve it to be just before God and Man.

   Given under our hands this 3rd September 1800.
James Roberson,Hundr. Ansel Zizer,Hundr.Isaac
Anderson,Hundr. and Nathl.Wansey,Chairman signed
this as a law in Sierra Leone.

40. Notice, 10 September 1800

September 10th 1800
                       This is to give notis that the law of
the Sierra leone Setler is to tak place the 25 of this
mounth. By the orders of the Hundred and tyding all
complant is to go of Be given in to James robenson ancel
Zyzer I Suck anderson Hundreds

41. Isaac Anderson, unsigned, undated

September Sunday Mr Ludlow Sir we we de sire to now wether you will let our Mends out if not turn out the womans and Chill Dren

The Notes

Notes on the Documents

Most of the following letters and petitions were sent to John Clarkson and are preserved in the collections of his papers in the British Library, London, and in the Sierra Leone Collection, Special Collections, The University Library, University of Illinois at Chicago. They are supplemented by documents copied verbatim into the minute books of the Governor's Council in the Public Record Office, London. They have been reproduced as written.

It is impossible to estimate how many Nova Scotians could read and write. Judging by the different handwriting, about thirty of them were responsible for the documents printed here. Some however were not written by those who signed them (e.g. Documents 19, 34 and probably 31). The first of the three letters written in London by Perkins and Anderson (Document 18) is in a different hand from the other two (Documents 20, 21) and all are different from Anderson's own letter (Document 22). Nor can one tell who wrote the multiple-authored letters and petitions.

Nor could all those whose names appear as signatories necessarily read and write. Some signed with a mark (X), some allowed others to sign for them. However, the use of a mark does not always connote being unable to read and write. Several literates' names appear on Document 12, but the names have all been written down in the same hand with a mark beside each. On Document 14 some have appended their signatures, others have had their names written down for them, with or without the addition 'his mark'.

Two are from women (Documents 4, 9). Some Nova Scotian women could read and write, indeed some were schoolteachers (see note on Document 5), but one cannot now tell whether these two letters were actually written by the women who sent them.

1. Birchtown People's Petition
(British Library, Add. MS 41262A fol. 23)

Clarkson wrote to Henry Thornton, Chairman of the Sierra Leone Company, that he would grant this petition, adding, 'I can assure you without the least enthusiasm [i.e. exaggeration] that the majority of these men are better than any people in the labouring line of life in England'. (New York Historical Society, John Clarkson's diary, 28 November 1791)

2. Thomas Peters and David Edmon, 23 December 1791
(Add. MS 41262A fol. 24)

Clarkson wrote in his diary, 'As the people here have hitherto conducted themselves not only to my wishes, but to the satisfaction of the whole Town, I promised them as a reward for their good behaviour that I should order the whole to have fresh Beef on Christmas Day, this pleased them very much'. (Clarkson's diary, 23 December 1791)

1. The people from Annapolis, Nova Scotia.

2. For Thomas Peters see *Introduction*. David Edmonds was captain of one of the companies. In Sierra Leone he was elected a tythingman in 1795 and hundredor in 1798. He supported the Company in 1800 and was badly wounded trying to arrest Nathaniel Wansey.

3. Peter Richardson, 12 January 1792
(Sierra Leone Collection, Special Collections, The University Library, University of Illinois at Chicago)

Written on board ship awaiting departure from Halifax. There is no comment on this letter in Clarkson's diary.

4. Susana Smith, 12 May 1792
(University of Illinois at Chicago)

Clarkson's diary doesn't record whether he supplied her with soap.

5. Richard Dickson, 15 May 1792
(University of Illinois at Chicago)

Clarkson's diary records no reaction to this letter. An elderly settler, Joseph Leonard, who had been a teacher in Nova Scotia, and his daughters Phoebe and Flora (later Mrs Eli Ackim) were appointed the first schoolteachers.

1. Richard Dickson (or Dixon) was employed as messenger and occasional clerk to the governor and council.

6. Daniel Cary, 16 June 1792
(University of Illinois at Chicago)

Clarkson's diary does not record whether he performed the ceremony.

7. Beverhout Company, 26 June 1792
(University of Illinois at Chicago)

For the context of the petition see *Introduction*, p. 7.

1. The paper with the Sierra Leone Company's terms which Clarkson took to Nova Scotia.

2. Henry Beverhout was born free in the Dutch colony of St Croix, but by the period of the American War was living in Charleston, South Carolina. In New Brunswick he organised a Methodist congregation which joined Clarkson in Halifax. They formed a company on board ship and stayed together in Sierra Leone. (See also Document 15.)

8. Andrew Moor, 24 August 1792
(University of Illinois at Chicago)

1. He invests Clarkson with the grandiose titles borne by the governors of British royal colonies.

2. Andrew Moore was born in Africa and taken as a slave to Georgia. In Sierra Leone he was granted good farmland above Freetown (near the present Leicester village) and was the first to discover indigenous coffee growing. In later life he became the official grave-digger and church clerk, retiring on pension in 1839, aged about 77.

9. Rose Morral, 5 November 1792
(University of Illinois at Chicago)

Clarkson wrote in his diary – 'November 5th. Rainy day. I was occupied a great part of the morning in trying to convince a woman that I had not the power to dissolve her marriage; she would persist that I might do it if I chose. I remember when I published the banns of marriage between her and her present husband, Murral, that I warned her of the step she was about to take, and told her how I knew it would end, and before I married them, I again advised them both to take some further time to think about it, for I was satisfied their tempers would not suit each other; but all to no purpose. I told the woman to return home, and I would take an opportunity of calling upon her husband, and of doing what I could to reconcile them to each other'.

10. Luke Jordan, 18 November 1792
(University of Illinois at Chicago)

For Clarkson's response see Document 12.

1. Luke Jordan, born in Virginia, was captain on board the *Brothers* ship and a leading elder in Moses Wilkinson's congregation. He was elected tythingman in 1796, 1797 and 1798. After that year his name no longer appears in the surviving records, so he may have then died. See also *Introduction* and Documents 23, 24, 25, 31.

11. John Cuthbert, 19 November 1792
(University of Illinois at Chicago)

1. John Cuthbert was a captain. Clarkson regarded him as one of the steadiest men in the colony. Subsequently he turned against the Company (see *Introduction* p. 16).

12. Petition (John Duncome and others), 19 November 1792
(University of Illinois at Chicago)

Clarkson compromised by continuing their existing pay and giving them credit at the Company's store in lieu of their weekly provisions. But he refused the request for more liquor, noting with sadness in his diary that whereas in Nova Scotia, and during the early days in Sierra Leone, there had been little drinking, drunkenness was now becoming common.

1. The Sierra Leone Company issued its own coinage – on one side a lion, on the other black and white hands clasped in friendship.
2. Perkins, Hogg, Peters, Webb, Johnson, Prophet and Sillavan (Sullivan) were captains.

13. Antson Zizer, 26 November 1792
(University of Illinois at Chicago)

There is no reference to this letter or any response in Clarkson's diary.

1. Antson (later written Ansel) Zizer, born in Africa, was one of the captains. He served regularly as a tythingman and hundredor and was active against the Company's government (see *Introduction*). Banished in 1800, he returned after the amnesty as a trader, and died in 1843 aged over 80. (His descendant J. C. Zizer, who died in 1959, practised as a lawyer in Lagos, and also made a name for himself in opposition to the colonial government.)

14. Farewell Petition, 28 November 1792
(University of Illinois at Chicago)

David George and Richard Corankeapoan (Crankapone) were two of the Company's most loyal supporters. But the petitioners also include some of its subsequent opponents: Stephen Peters (Document 24), Isaac Streeter (Document 35) and Francis Patrick who was hanged in 1800.

15. Beverhout Company, 11 December 1792
(Add. MS 41262A fol. 209)

The episode mentioned here is not referred to in Clarkson's diary or in any other surviving document. Clarkson appointed Beverhout Church Clerk to keep him quiet, but he was later dismissed for improper behaviour with a schoolgirl. The last documentary reference to him is dated 1797.

16. Richard Corankeapoan
(University of Illinois at Chicago)

1. For DuBois see note on Document 18.
2. Clarkson had taken David George on a visit to England to meet fellow Baptists.
3. For John Cuthbert see note on Document 11.
4. For Corankeapoan (Crankapone) see *Introduction*. As a final act of service, he was killed defending Freetown during King Tom's attack in 1801.

17. Miles Dixon, 14 October 1793
(University of Illinois at Chicago)

1. David George, having been well treated by the Sierra Leone Company directors on his visit to London, seems to have taken their side against Clarkson.

2. Miles Dixon was employed by the Company as schoolmaster, and held other official posts (e.g. Document 37). He was regularly elected a tythingman, and strongly opposed quit–rents, but took no part in the rebellion.

18. Cato Perkins and Isaac Anderson, 26 October 1793
(Add. MS 41263 fol. 97)

For the context of Documents 18–22 see *Introduction*, p. 9.

1. Isaac DuBois, one of the Company's employees, was a white Loyalist from North Carolina who had known some of the settlers in childhood. He was one of Clarkson's allies and was also dismissed in 1793. He seems to have given Perkins and Anderson some help in drawing up the petition.

   In Sierra Leone he had married Anna Maria Falconbridge who on her return to England published *Two Voyages to Sierra Leone* (London, 1794, reprinted 1795, 1803 and 1967) bitterly denouncing the directors. During the quit–rent dispute in 1797 Anderson produced a copy of the book and quoted it against Zachary Macaulay.

2. Perkins and Anderson were both born in Charleston, South Carolina, Perkins as a slave, Anderson free. Perkins was never elected hundredor or tythingman (the pastors seem not to have stood for election), and though some of his congregation were involved in the rebellion, he took no part. He died in 1805. Anderson was to lead the rebellion (*Introduction*, pp. 17–19).

19. Settlers' Petition
(Add. MS 41263 fols. 98–100)

The petition is a fair copy, not written by Perkins or Anderson.

1. The signatures do not appear on the copy in the Clarkson papers.

20. Cato Perkins and Isaac Anderson, 30 October 1793
(Add. MS 41263 fol. 101)

The handwriting of Documents 20, 21 and 22 differs from that of Document 18.

1. Selina, Countess of Huntingdon, had died in 1791. They refer here to her successor Lady Ann Erskine.

21. Isaac Anderson and Cato Perkins, 9 November 1793
(Add. MS 41263 fol. 105)

22. Isaac Anderson, 11 February 1794
(Add MS 41263 fols. 108–9)

The handwriting is not the same as that of Documents 18, 20, 21.

1. See *Introduction*, p. 10.
2. The Sierra Leone House was the Company's headquarters in London.

23. Luke Jordan and Isaac Anderson, 28 June 1794
(Add. MS 41263 fol. 112)

1. See *Introduction*, p. 10.

2. See *Introduction*, p. 9.

3. See note on Document 10.

24. Luke Jordan and others, 19 November 1794
(Add. MS 41263 fols. 114–5)

1. See *Introduction*, p. 11.

2. The names appended (not signatures, but written down by the writer of the letter) were those of members of Moses Wilkinson's Methodist congregation. Wilkinson, a blind and lame preacher from Virginia, was passionate in the pulpit. Clarkson, hearing him in Birchtown, wrote, 'he worked himself up to such a pitch that I was fearful something would happen to him' (Clarkson's diary, 13 December 1791), and an English Methodist missionary wrote of him in 1813, 'he outstretches his voice at times to terror and frightfulness'. (Methodist Missionary Society Archives, *Sierra Leone*, no. 88, Healey, 24 April 1813.)

   America Talbot and Stephen Peters were ruling elders of the congregation – Peters, according to Zachary Macaulay, 'one of their great thundering orators' (Huntington Library, California, Zachary Macaulay's journal, 21 December 1796). Tolbert left the colony for the Pirates' Bay settlement. Peters, regularly elected a tythingman until 1800, took no part in the rebellion. Rubin Simmons however took an active part. He managed to evade capture and lived for several years outside the colony, but was eventually allowed to return.

25. Sundry Settlers, 16 April 1795
(Public Record Office, CO 270/3 fols. 72–4)

For the context of Documents 25, 26 see *Introduction*, p. 11.

1. Nathaniel Snowball, originally from Virginia, was a leading member of Moses Wilkinson's congregation. He led the exodus to Pirates' Bay where he was regarded as governor (Document 30). He returned to the colony during the Temne war and died soon after.

2. Jonathan Glasgow, another of Moses Wilkinson's elders, was also from Virginia and a leader at Pirates' Bay. His name appears on no record after 1796.

26. Settlers, 22 April 1795
(CO 270/3 fol. 76)

27. John Cooper, 14 January 1796
(Add. MS 41263 fol. 119)

1. John Cooper subsequently left the colony for Pirates' Bay.

28. James Liaster, 30 March 1796
(Add. MS 41263 fols. 120–1)

1. Prince George and Jemmy Queen were the Temne rulers who controlled Pirates' (or Cockle) Bay.

2. James Liaster (or Lester), born in Carolina, was one of the Preston people (Document 1). He settled at Pirates' Bay.

29. James Hutcherson and Moses Murray, 24 May 1796
(Add. MS 41263 fol. 127)

1. James Hutcherson (or Hutchinson) was a member of Moses Wilkinson's congregation.

2. Moses Murray, born in Virginia, was one of the Birchtown people. He died in Freetown in 1802.

30. Nathaniel Snowball and James Hutcherson, 24 May 1796
(Add. MS 41263 fol. 129)

31. Luke Jordan and Nathaniel Snowball, 29 July 1796
(Add. MS 41263 fol. 131)

This letter is different from the others in style and in handwriting. It may have been written on behalf of Jordan and Snowball by John Garvin, a white Methodist schoolmaster, or by Jacob Grigg, a white Baptist missionary, both of whom disliked the Company's government, to stir up sectarian strife.

1. See *Introduction*, p. 13.

2. Moses Wilkinson.

32. Boston King, 1 June 1797
(Add. MS 41263 fol. 147)

In reply to this letter Clarkson sent the paper and pens he asked for, also a gold-laced hat to be given to one of the neighbouring African chiefs.

He added some advice to the settlers: 'you must not quarrel with each other, or with your Rulers, but put up with little inconveniences to insure the future happiness of your posterity'.

1. Cockle Bay was the alternative name for Pirates' Bay.

2. Boston King, from Charleston, South Carolina, carpenter and boat-builder, became a Methodist preacher in Nova Scotia and joined Clarkson in the hope of becoming a missionary in Africa. When the Sierra Leone Company started a plantation across the estuary on the Bulom Shore he settled there, preached and opened a small school. In 1794 the Company brought him to England for more education. While there he dictated a narrative of his life which was printed in the *Methodist Magazine* (volume 21, 1798). On his return he taught in the school in Freetown, but may eventually have resumed his missionary vocation since he died in the Sherbro country about 1802.

33. Boston King, 16 January 1798
(Add. MS 41263 fols. 149–50)

1. Signior Domingo, the recipient of Clarkson's hat, was of Afro-Portuguese origin, and ruled at Royema along the shore east of the colony.

2. Samuel Whitbread MP, a wealthy brewer, took an interest in Sierra Leone, though not a director of the Company.

3. Henry Thornton was chairman of the board of directors of the Sierra Leone Company. Because Boston King went to visit Clarkson on his visit to England Thornton made him pay his own passage back to Sierra Leone, after having promised him a free passage.

34. Isaac Anderson, 21 January 1798
(Add. MS 41263 fol. 151)

The letter is in Boston King's handwriting. He has written Anderson's first name 'Isaiah' instead of Isaac.

1. The quotation 'Thou shalt not muzzle the ox that treadeth out the corn' is from the Bible, Deuteronomy XXV, 4.

2. The pamphlet is a printed address by Macaulay urging the people to pay quit–rent (a copy is stuck into CO 270/4).

3. Neither Professor Paul Edwards nor the editor can elucidate 'Peter Corner'. It is plainly a satirical reference to Macaulay.

35. Isaac Streeter and George Carrol, 5 August 1797
(CO 270/4 fol. 90)

For the context see *Introduction* p. 14.

1. Isaac Streeter and George Carrol, regularly elected hundredor or tythingman, were regarded by the Company's officials as disaffected. Macaulay, comparing Carrol with Anderson described him as 'more hot and passionate and more ignorant'. (Zachary Macaulay's journal, 21 December 1796). But neither took any part in the rebellion.

36. Ishmael York, Stephen Peters and Isaac Anderson, 16 January 1798
(CO 270/4 fols. 103–4)

Captain H. L. Ball, commanding HMS *Daedalus*, called at Freetown in January 1798 and was given this letter which he passed on to Macaulay without replying to it.

1. Ishmael York, born in Carolina, was a Huntingdonian elder. He was regularly elected hundredor or tythingman, and tried vainly in 1796 to prevent whites standing for election. He was himself deprived of his hundredorship after losing a case against another settler whom he had accused of witchcraft. He supported Robertson and Wansey (Document 38), and though he took no active part in the rebellion was banished from the colony.

37. Resolutions of the Hundredors and Tythingmen, August–September 1799
(CO 270/4 fols. 151–2)

1. Granville Town, east of Freetown, was occupied by the survivors of the original 1787 settlement founded by Granville Sharp and formed part of the colony.

2. James Robertson, born in Virginia, was one of the captains. He had a grievance over a lawsuit he had failed to win, and when he was elected a tythingman in 1798 insisted on the people's right to choose their own judges, and make their own laws. He was chosen judge and signed the Paper of Laws (Document 39). Arrested at the beginning of the fighting, he was found guilty of rebellion and banished to Gorée.

3. Nathaniel Wansey, from Pennsylvania, farmed on the hill above Freetown, later Tower Hill. Elected a tythingman in 1798, he associated himself with Robertson and signed the Paper of Laws. He evaded arrest, and joined Anderson in armed rebellion. Subsequently he took refuge with neighbouring Temne rulers and may have taken part in King Tom's assaults on Freetown in 1801 and 1802. He then moved north to the Melakori country where he was handed over in chains to the colony authorities. No record of his fate survives.

4. See Document 17, note 2.

5. Thomas Freeman, one of Moses Wilkinson's elders, was elected a hundredor in 1798. There is no record of him in any document after 1799 so he may have died before the outbreak of the rebellion.

38. Nathaniel Wansey, 13 February 1800
(CO 270/5 fols. 151–2)

For the context see *Introduction*, p. 17.

1. 'I' is James Robertson.

2. The war between Britain and France had brought many more British naval ships to Freetown.

39. Paper of Laws, 3 September 1800
(CO 270/5 Narrative of the Rebellion, pp. 98–9)

For the context see *Introduction* p. 17.

1. Abram Smith was banished after the rebellion but returned to the colony with the amnesty.

2. The contraction '/–' stands for shilling, 'd.' for pence.

3. abort.

40. Notice, 10 September 1800
(270/5 Narrative, Appendix No. 3)

41. Isaac Anderson, unsigned, undated
(CO270/5 Narrative, Appendix No. 8)

Isaac Anderson's unsigned letter was his death warrant. The charter of justice granted by the British crown did not empower the Company to prosecute for treason. To avoid the expense of organising a treason trial in London, he was instead charged with one of the numerous statutory offences which under English law at that date carried the death penalty – sending an anonymous and threatening letter to the governor. Francis Patrick similarly was hanged 'for feloniously taking and carrying away a gun', also a capital offence.

Appendix: Some grammatical characteristics of the Sierra Leone letters

by Charles Jones

In their efforts to recover the features of past grammars, historical linguists have made scant use of the evidence provided by the non-standard orthographic conventions of uneducated or partly educated writers. Together with information from dialectal sources, such materials have very often been accorded a status only appropriate for the provision of 'exceptional' or exotic materials, and what has been seen as mainline grammatical (especially phonological) development has been deduced from the evidence of poetic rhymes and the direct comments and specialised phonetic alphabet systems of grammarians.

This state of affairs is especially prevalent when materials of a sixteenth to nineteenth-century provenance have been examined and the foundation of our knowledge of pronunciation habits and syntactic usage has rested upon the (often very sophisticated) observations of 'orthoepists' such as Gill, Hart and Robinson, foreign language grammar writers like Salesbury and Flint as well as dictionary makers such as Walker and Johnson among many others (Dobson, 1968; Ekwall, 1975; Zachrisson, 1913). While well-known and substantial collections of such materials exist – notably the *The Diary of Henry Machyn, Citizen and Merchant-Taylor of London* (Nichols, 1848), the seventeenth-century *Verney Papers* (Verney and Verney, 1925) and in a North American context, J. R. Lowell's *The Biglow Papers*, 1880 – whenever non-standard or 'naive' orthographic systems have been turned to, they have tended to have assigned to them only the value of 'occasional' spellings and their possible systematic characteristics have by and large been ignored (but see Wyld, 1936; Osselton, 1977; Matthews, 1936a, 1936b; Bartsch, 1987).

The Sierra Leone Settlers' Letters provide a unique and

extensive collection of non-standard orthographic representations of the form of English spoken by black North American
ex-slaves at the close of the eighteenth century. They offer an
opportunity to reveal the extent to which the language of
these speakers differed from or was similar to that of their
white contemporaries and even to appraise the extent to
which that language could be described as belonging to some
point on a scale of creolisation. Although the materials in
the settlers' letters deserve a much fuller treatment than is
possible here, we shall try to suggest that they are illustrative
of a linguistic usage which is not significantly unlike that
which we might expect from contemporary lower class white
American English speakers and which shows no unambiguous
evidence of being in a creole or any other pre-natural
language state.

While materials providing evidence for the earliest forms of
the English Language in North America are relatively scarce
(Mathews, 1931; Alleyne, 1974; Cade, 1935; Combs, 1916;
Orbeck, 1927) those describing the unique characteristics
(if, indeed, there were any) of the English spoken by black
speakers in the earliest period of the European settlement of
that continent are even more sparse (Dillard, 1971, 1972,
1973; Cruikshank, 1910; Read 1933). The importance of
the settlers' letters as a source for such evidence cannot be
overestimated especially since, as we shall attempt to show,
the non-standard orthographic forms they contain are highly
systematic and non-random.

The linguistic origins of the English used by black slaves in
colonial North America has been the subject of considerable
debate and Dillard (notably 1972 and 1985) espouses most
strongly the view that Black American English has a different
source from the 'transplanted' British English of the white
colonists. That source, it is claimed, lies in pidgin and
creolised versions of English, especially those originating in
West Africa and spread in a 'maritime' pidgin or creole form
throughout the eastern and southern seaboard of the North
American landmass. And indeed there is evidence to suggest

the existence from the eighteenth century (and perhaps earlier) of a 'Guinea Coast Creole English' spoken not only in West Africa, but in use by slaves in the North American colonies themselves (Hancock, 1986).

Two pieces of evidence in the Clarkson papers show that some of the settlers did speak a form of creolised English. In his rough notebook Clarkson jotted down an unattributed remark, 'Massa Governor no mind king. he no mind you' (Add. MS 41262B fol. 9).

And in his diary, under date 2 November 1791, he recorded the following conversation with one of the prospective settlers:

> ... he came originally from the coast of Africa, and spoke English indifferently: the following dialogue passed between us – 'Well my friend I suppose you are thoroughly acquainted with the nature of the proposals offered to you by His Majesty' – 'No Massa me no hear, nor no mind, me work like slave, cannot do worse Massa in any part of the world, therefore am determined to goo with you Massa if you please' – 'You must consider that this [*sic*] a new Settlement, and should you keep your health must expect to meet with many difficulties, if you engage in it' – 'Me well know that Massa, me can work much, and care not for climate; if me die, me die, had rather die in me own Country than in this cold place'.

As Clarkson explicitly mentioned that the speaker had been brought from Africa and had not, like most of the other settlers, been born in North America, one can infer that he had already learnt Guinea Coast Creole English in West Africa. In this regard one may refer also to Zachary Macaulay's journal (under dates 11 June 1796, 13 May 1796). When he quoted settlers verbatim they use ordinary English (e.g. Moses Wilkinson, 'I have worship in my family before daylight every morning'). But Africans he quoted verbatim were recorded in a creolised English (e.g. King Jimmy, 'I thank you too much for them people you bring from American vessel').

What we shall try to demonstrate is that the language of the Sierra Leone letters, far from representing some kind of pidgin or even advanced pidgin (creolised) version of 'real' English, manifests many of the features of late eighteenth-century American and, indeed, British English. We shall conclude that the English of these letters is a fairly typical example of North American English from the period, although probably that of the lower social classes, both white and black. To assist us towards a conclusion like this, we shall demonstrate that most of especially the phonological characteristics of the writers of the settlers' letters can be shown to have existed in contemporary or near contemporary North American lower class white speech as well as in the language of their British counterparts.

For data for the former we shall make special reference to the materials in the *List of Provincialisms* in the Rev. Adiel Sherwood's *Gazetteer of the State of Georgia* (1827) (Mathews, 1931) and the glossary added to David Humphreys' drama *The Yankee in England* (1815) where are to be found 'words used in a particular sense, in this Drama; or pronounced with an accent or emphasis in certain districts, differing from the modes generally followed by the inhabitants of the United States; including new-coined American, obsolete English, and low words in general' (Mathews, 1931). An excellent source too for 'improper provincialisms and vulgarisms' is Samuel Kirkham's *English Grammar in Familiar Lectures* (Rochester, 1833). For contemporary British English materials we shall appeal to George Jackson's *Popular Errors of English Grammar Particularly of Pronunciation* (London, 1830) and J. Walker's *A Critical Pronouncing Dictionary and Expositor of the English Language* (London, 1791).

A short essay like this can only select what appear to be the most interesting pointers to the grammatical output of the writers of the settlers' letters and we shall confine our comments to the areas of phonology and syntax/morphology. The letters which make up this collection range from those written almost exclusively in a standard orthographic form (Documents 17, 21, 23, 38, 39 and notably 19, the *Settlers' Petition*) to those where the writer has only the slightest grasp of standard spelling conventions and clearly innovates in his attempt to give the sounds of his language some kind of written representation (notably Documents 7, 14, 28, 29, 32, 33).

The interpretation of such non-standard spelling shapes is notoriously difficult but it is important to realise from the outset that we are clearly not dealing with some 'free-for-all' situation – spelling variation is constrained to a limited set of possibilities, and those variations themselves appear to reflect a restricted type of phonetic/phonological alternation, itself of a kind which we might readily expect for the historical period and (although there are difficult cases) typical of what we might recognise as the product of general phonological change in English (Jones, 1989; Lass, 1984: pp. 315–38). Syntactic peculiarities are likewise limited to a small number of types although their extent may be disguised by the stylistic and discourse structure peculiarities of the authors. The importance of these observations is that they suggest that non-standard orthographies, far from being the unconstrained mis-interpretations of standard models, can be seen as systematic attempts by writers to utilise what orthographic knowledge they possess in a rule governed way to express their phonological and phonetic intuitions and therefore be viewed as individual 'solutions' to the problem of finding an appropriate alphabetic representation for speech sounds.

PHONOLOGICAL PECULIARITIES OF THE SIERRA LEONE SETTLERS' LETTERS

It would, of course, take a study considerably longer than this to set out the range of criteria that might be proposed to justify our assigning to one kind of spelling shape a phonetic significance that we might want to deny another. Not only

that, but we should ideally wish to spend considerable effort
in supporting the phonetic value we decide to assign particular orthographic representations: what, for instance, (if any)
significance do the various manifestations in the settlers'
letters for *Sierra Leone* itself have for contemporary pronunciation:

‹Sira Lone›	(Document 22)
‹Sierra Leone›	(Documents 23, 24, 26)
‹Sierra Leona›	(Document 1)
‹Sirealeone›	(Document 15)
‹Saraleon›	(Document 7)

Are we to interpret data like these as evidence for a non-
diphthongal stressed vowel space such as [sɪrə] and [lon] or
even for pronunciations for the item as [sɪrəleon]? A question like this is far from easy to answer authoritatively and
we have not the space to examine all the possible criteria for
orthographic interpretation (Vachek, 1973): our observations
in the materials which follow will be of a very general kind
and the reader must be aware that they represent only a
selection of the possibilities available.

We might begin by observing that many of the non-
standard spelling representations in our data seem to show
something akin to phonetic alphabet-like attempts to represent pronunciation features. Consider the following
instances:

‹the›	*'they'*	(22)
‹wonce›	*'once'*	(24)
‹helth›	*'health'*	(23)
‹chuse›	*'choose'*	(19)
‹consern›	*'concern'*	(19)
‹sufficantly›	*'sufficiently'*	(36)
‹ranglesome›	*'wranglesome'*	(25)
‹suckcess›	*'success'*	(33)
‹Parlament›	*'Parliament'*	(26)
‹goverment›	*'government'*	(28)

‹govener›	*'governer'*	(7)
‹tarataras›	*'territories'*	(7)
‹produse›	*'produce'*	(7)

Although we should not be prepared, on every occasion, to take such forms at their face value, it would not seem too counter-intuitive to conclude that the above represent attempts to produce phonetic spellings for items whose 'standard' orthographic representations do not, in some way or another, show a one to one match between symbol and sound. However, there appear also to be instances where the presence of a non-standard orthographic shape is used where little or no appeal can be made to phonetic matching, and where the alternations look to be quite random, consider:

‹Ading›	*'adding'*	(29)
‹Writting›	*'writing'*	(29)
‹happyness›	*'happiness'*	(30)
‹Pleace›	*'please'*	(19)
‹wishe›	*'wish'*	(22)
‹tacke›	*'take'*	(22)
‹here›	*'hear'*	(28)

and many others. Indeed, 'naive' spellings not dissimilar to these are attested from North American sources from the mid-seventeenth century, as can be seen from shapes such as ‹absenc› *'absence'*, ‹pec› *'piece'*, ‹elc› *'else'*, ‹sariant› *'sergeant'* from the *Early New Haven Records (1637–87)* (Mathews, 1931: pp. 5–6). Yet there are several distinct sets of what can only be described as regular 'non-standard' orthographic practices to be observed throughout the settlers' letters which plainly capture contemporary phonological variation and alternation and which can be used to tell us a great deal both about the actual pronunciation habits of the writers and the sociolinguistic status of many of those habits. We shall concentrate on a half dozen or so of these, paying especial attention to the evidence the orthography provides for the behaviour of stressed vowels in sonorant consonant (particularly

[m]/[n]/[r]) contexts, the state of long stressed vowels in relation to *Great Vowel Shift* developments, the treatment of syllable final consonantal clusters and metathesis phenomena.

VOCALIC CHARACTERISTICS

Stressed vowels in pre-sonorant consonant environments

This environment is perhaps one of the most typical both in contemporary English and throughout the language's history for the production of certain kinds of effects on the vowel space before it. We regularly find changes involving length, diphthongisation as well as raisings and lowerings in vowel height when stressed syllables are terminated by (such highly vowel-like) segments as [r], [l], [m], [n], [ŋ] (Jones, 1989: pp. 141–66; pp. 236–52). Perhaps the most recurrent feature of the non-standard spelling in the settlers' letters is its tendency to show *pre-nasal vowel lowering*, especially involving the front vowels [ɪ] and [ɛ] which appear to be systematically lowered (made more sonorant, or [a]-like) when their syllable is terminated by a nasal sonorant, thus:

‹senceer›	*'sincere'*	(22)
‹empression›	*'impression'*	(24, 25)
‹enteligence›	*'intelligence'*	(24)
‹entention›	*'intention'*	(27)
‹emprision›	*'imprison'*	(26)
‹enquery›	*'inquiry'*	(26)
‹wane›	*'when'*	(22)
‹silant›	*'silent'*	(22)
‹consarned›	*'concerned'*	(22)
‹Lawrance›	*'Lawrence'*	(14)
‹wemen›	*'women'*	(14)
‹sence›	*'since'*	(16)

while Sherwood (1837) records ‹hender› *'hinder'* and ‹rench› *'rinse'*. At first sight paradoxically, such a post vocalic environment also triggers what looks to be the opposite process of vowel *raising*, such that [ɛ] palatalizes to [ɪ] or even [i], thus:

‹presint›	*'present'*	(32)
‹rin›	*'rain'*	(32)
‹sining›	*'sending'*	(33)
‹imbarque›	*'embark'*	(1)

Humphreys (1815) recording ‹frind› *'friend'*, ‹Gineral› *'general'* and ‹Gineration› *'generation'*, Sherwood (1837) noting ‹inimy› *'enemy'*. However, we should not be too puzzled by such anomalous behaviour since the [ɛ]/[ɪ] alternation in nasal contexts is well recorded and seems to reflect the fact that in the acoustically relatively noisy environment of the nasal segment, speakers will either raise or lower vowel segments to improve their opportunities of being perceived (Ohala, 1974: pp. 353–90).

There seems little doubt from the orthographic evidence of these letters that the phonology of their writers was fully rhotic: post vocalic [r] was still generally realised and triggering changes in its immediate environment which are well documented in every historical period in the language. The commonest of these in our data is the propensity for vowel lowering in syllables terminated by [r], mainly where an etymological [ɛ] surfaces as [æ]. Consider the following typical cases:

Settlers' letters	Humphreys	Sherwood	Jackson
‹consarned› (22)	‹concarning›	‹arrant›	‹sartain›
‹marcy› (22)	‹marcy›	‹marcy›	‹sarvant›
‹sarvant› (22)	‹sarvant›	‹marchant›	‹larn›
‹farme› (32)	‹larning›	‹obsarvar›	
‹Amaraca› (2, 7)	‹atarnal›		
‹desarving› (25)	‹sarvice›		
	‹sarpent›		
	‹varses›		

and many others. This pre-[r] [æ]/[ɛ] alternation is attested early in the language's history: cf. such fifteenth-century spelling alternations as ‹sergeant›/‹sargeant›, ‹certain›/‹sartan›, ‹herte›/‹hart›,   ‹sermon›/‹sarmoun›,   ‹servaunt›/‹sarvaunt› (Jones, 1989: pp. 246–7; Berndt, 1960: pp. 70–2). That versions with the lowered vowel are clearly stigmatised in the late eighteenth century and early nineteenth century in United States white English is suggested by the inclusion of the forms listed above in Humphreys' and Sherwood's lists, while their potential for giving offence to polite London usage is clear from Jackson's (1830) condemnation of pronunciations such as *sartain, sarvant* and *larn* among others.

The strong rhotic nature of the speech of the writers of the settlers' letters can be inferred through the operation of such lowering processes as well as from the fact that there appears to be only a few occasions where their orthographic habits show post vocalic [r] to have been effaced: ‹yea› *'year'* (Document 32), perhaps representing some kind of [jeə] pronunciation with the diphthongisation triggered, as we might expect, by the [r] effacement, and ‹honnah› *'honour'* (Documents 10, 11). Nevertheless, this apparent lack of [r] deletion post vocalically is somewhat surprising since, as we have observed above, there are some characteristics of the writers' orthography which seem to reveal that their speech contained socially stigmatised elements. At the end of the eighteenth century, *effacement* of post vocalic [r] (such a salient feature of polite southern British English) was apparently regarded as characteristic of speakers from the lower echelons of society. Jackson (1830), for instance, warns his readers against such a practice, condemning pronunciations such as (cawn) *'corn'*, (cuss) *'curse'*, (nuss) *'nurse'*, (gaal) *'girl'*, (hawse) *'horse'*, while Flint (Kökeritz, 1944: p. 41) who is one of the first phoneticians systematically to record post vocalic [r] effacement, strongly suggests that in the second half of the eighteenth century its use was confined to a rather limited set in the lexicon (Jones, 1989: p. 300). Certainly Walker's (1791) comments on the innovation hardly recommend it to his subscribers:

In England, and particularly in London, the *r* in *lard, bard,*

card, regard, &c is pronounced so much in the throat as
to be little more than the middle or Italian *a*, lengthened
into *baa, baad, caad, regaad*; while in Ireland, the *r*, in
these words, is pronounced with so strong a jar of the tongue
against the forepart of the palate, and accompanied with such
an aspiration or strong breathing at the beginning of the
letter, as to produce that harshness we call the Irish accent.
But if the letter is too forcibly pronounced in Ireland, it
is often too feebly sounded in London where it is sometimes
entirely sunk.

That our letter writers appear to avoid such a 'sinking' of
post vocalic [r] might reflect their consciousness of the
stigmatised nature of the process, making it inappropriate for
the relatively formal nature of the written discourse they were
attempting to produce. Their reticence to use [r]-less types is
all the more puzzling, given the fairly strong attestation of
such forms in both Humphreys and Sherwood:

Humphreys		*Sherwood*	
⟨cuss⟩	*'curse'*	⟨scace⟩	*'scarce'*
⟨cussed⟩	*'cursed'*	⟨erro⟩	*'error'*
⟨hoss⟩	*'horse'*	⟨gal⟩	*'girl'*
⟨massiful⟩	*'merciful'*	⟨hath⟩	*'hearth'*
		⟨impotent⟩	*'important'*
		⟨pillow⟩	*'pillar'*
		⟨terra⟩	*'terror'*

Yet the same cannot be said of the Nova Scotian realisation
of that other, also highly stigmatised, manifestation of post
vocalic [r]: where it is 'inserted' unhistorically to the right of
the stressed vowel. Consider the following samples:

⟨James Hutcherson⟩	*'Hutchinson'*	(29)
⟨larst⟩	*'last'*	(2)
⟨persesion⟩	*'possession'*	(26)
⟨satterfaction⟩	*'satisfaction'*	(33)
⟨Corlector⟩	*'collector'*	(37)

‹wherther›	*'whether'*	(7)
‹ragerlations›	*'regulations'*	(7)
‹wagers›	*'wages'*	(7)
‹drowr›	*'draw'*	(7)
‹Partrick›	*'Patrick'*	(14)
‹wors›	*'was'*	(14)
‹parshige›	*'passage'*	(14)

and perhaps too in instances such as ‹we hear your are amongst the best People in England› (Document 19) and ‹your will be pleased› (Document 7). Such intrusive [r] constructions are, of course, a feature of much modern southern British English – [læst tæŋgər ɪn pærɪs] *'Last Tango in Paris'* (Wells, 1982: pp. 222–7) and again regarded by Humphreys, Sherwood (where they are particularly common) and Jackson as socially unacceptable (Jones, 1989: pp. 300–1).

Sherwood		Humphreys		Jackson	
‹dairter›	*'daughter'*			‹darter	
‹arter›	*'after'*	‹fort›	*'fault'*	‹dorn›	*'dawn'*
‹feller›	*'fellow'*	‹sairse›	*'sauce'*	‹sarsepan›	
‹discurse›	*'discourse'*	‹borrerd›	*'borrowed'*		
‹fermiliar›	*'familiar'*				
‹pertition›	*'petition'*				
‹tater›	*'potato'*				
‹yaller›	*'yellow'*				

Vowel Shift Effects

One of the most prominent characteristics of historical English phonology lies in the language's treatment of stressed vowels which show extended durational characteristics. From as early as perhaps the fifteenth century there is a tendency for such vowels to 'shift'; essentially this involves vowels which are neither the pure palatal [ii] or labial [uu] losing their sonority ([a]) characteristic and targeting towards either palatality/labiality pole. Thus (in an extremely simplified form) we find developments like:

13th century	15th century	16th–18th century	
[ææ] ‹hær›	[ɛɛ] ‹heer›	[ee] ‹hair›	*'hair'*
	[ɛɛ] ‹se›	[ee] ‹say›	*'say'*
	[ee] ‹see›	[ii] ‹sea›	*'sea'*
	[ɔɔ] ‹home›	[oo] ‹home›	*'home'*
	[oo] ‹foot›	[uu] ‹foot›	*'foot'*

While such a display is a gross oversimplification both of the dating for the phenomenon, the way it applies to individual items and the precise phonetic realisations characteristic of the dates cited, it still serves to show the general 'raising' effect undergone by long stressed vowels in the language's history. One idiosyncracy of this effect lies in the fact that the shifting does not occur uniformly either throughout the temporal span or across dialectal areas; for instance, it is clear that for many British English speakers there has been a raising of the early [ee] to [ii] in an item like '*meat*', and of [ɛɛ] to [ee] (with subsequent diphthongisation to [ei]) in one like '*mate*'. However, in some Irish English dialects, the former has remained unshifted at [meet] and there has been some kind of '*meat*'/'*mate*' merger (Harris, 1985; Jones, 1989: pp. 283–92). While it is notoriously difficult to state with certainty the precise phonetic values of vowel symbols in materials like the settlers' letters, there appears to be some evidence (although it must be regarded as very tentative) that for some lexical items the vowel shift raising effect we have outlined above had not yet reached the 'stage' we associate with the modern language.

Modern British English				
[ee]/[eɪ]	[ii]	[oo]/[ou]	[aɪ]	[au]
Settlers' letters				
‹naims› (32)	‹this› (16)	‹thuse› (26)	‹Oblidge› (12)	
‹thay› (25, 26)	‹chef› (17)		‹complyed› (26)	
‹grate› (32)	‹peice› (25)		‹appleyed› (36)	
‹mad› (33)	‹greaf› (29)			
‹gratter› (33)	‹senceer› (21)			
‹trator› (15)	‹clair› (37)			
‹thea› (16)	‹cleained› (37)			
‹lad› (13)				
‹obay› (14)				
‹remander› (14)				
Sherwood				
‹et›	‹beneth›			
‹Jemes›	‹beneath›			
‹keerless›	‹cheer›			
	‹et›			
	‹rared›			
Humphreys				
‹saie›	‹beleve›	‹clus›		‹keows›
‹strait›	‹farce›	‹hull›		
	‹fairce›	‹hum›		
	‹railly›	‹humbly›		
1	2	3	4	5

While the ‹a›/‹ai›/‹ay›/‹ea› spellings in the first column are open to a number of interpretations, some writers believe that they may represent [εε] pronunciations, the 'stage' before the later raising to [ee] and (in some dialects, diphthongisation to [ei]) (Matthews (1936)), indicating late eighteenth-century forms such as [rεεlɪ], [nεεmz], [ðεε], [grεεt] and so on. While such spellings are common for the settlers' letters and evidenced too in Humphreys, it is interesting to note their absence in the later Sherwood, where [ee] pronunciations might be indicated. All three sources show (what are presumably stigmatised) [εε] pronunciations in column two items as well – [klεεr] *'clear'*, [rεεrd] *'reared'*, [bənεεθ] *'beneath'*, although the presence of spellings like ‹chef› *'chief'* and ‹cheer› *'cheer'*, might just indicate [ťeef]/[ťeer] pronuncia-tions, while those in the settlers' letters with ‹–i› final di-graphs – ‹peice› *'peace'* and ‹cleaned› *'cleaned'* could just possibly be interpreted as showing that raising was occurring here too, perhaps not to the extent of [ii], but to some more palatal version of [ee], i.e. [ęę].

A well attested effect of this vowel shift process upon pure palatal and labial long vowels like [ii] and [uu] was one of diphthongisation: cf. the modern [main] *'mine'* and [haus] *'house'* reflexes of pre-fifteenth century English [miin] and [huus]. Perhaps column four spellings such as ‹oblidge› *'oblige'* (Documents 12, 27) and ‹complyed› *'complied'* (Docu-ment 25) (as against the ‹appleyed› *'applied'* spelling in Document 36) suggest pre-diphthongal shapes like [obliidʒd], [kəmpliid]. But there is evidence too that the vowel shift had, for our writers, perhaps gone further than its modern southern British 'standard' version. Spellings such as ‹how› *'who'* (Document 37), ‹youse› *'use'* (Document 37) and perhaps ‹ashoure› *'assure'* might just point to [ɔu] or [au] stressed vowel pronunciations. Likewise, a spelling such as ‹thuse› *'those'* could even indicate an [oo] to [uu] vowel shift raising unachieved by most modern varieties of the language (Dobson, 1968: p. 676), a development especially evident in the column three stigmatised instances from Humphreys, where we find ‹clus› *'close'*, ‹hull› *'whole'*, ‹hum› *'home'* and ‹humbly› *'homely'* (Kirkham's (1833) ‹humble›).

The [ɔɪ] Diphthong

For whatever reason or sets of reasons (and the issue is a complex one), the diphthong [ɔɪ] (as in *'boy'*) comes to be conflated with [əɪ]/[aɪ] at a very early period in the history of the English language (probably as early as the fifteenth century) – cf. such rhymes as Spenser's ‹toyle›/‹compile›, Swift's ‹toil›/‹pile› and ‹join›/‹divine›/‹line› (Wyld, 1936: sect. 270; Dobson, 1968: sect. 258). This conflation is still evident in several modern British English dialects, notably those in west central Scotland, where we find pronunciations such as [spəil] '*spoil*', [bəil] '*boil*' and [əil] '*oil*' (Houston and Eaglesham, Renfrewshire) alongside such 'etymological' [əi] containing words as [fəil] '*file*' and [məil] '*mile*' (Mather and Speitel, 1986: pp. 130–1). That such [əi] for [ɔi] realisations were regarded as socially unacceptable in the late eighteenth century is clear from Walker's (1791) remark:

> OI. The general, and almost universal sound of this diphthong is that of *a* in *water*, and the first *e* of *me-tre*. This double sound is very distinguishable in *boil*, *toil*, *spoil*, *joint*, *point*, *anoint*, &c, which sound ought to be carefully preserved, as there is a very prevalent practice among the vulgar of dropping the *o*, and pronouncing these words as if written *bile*, *tile*, *spile*, etc.

Consider the following data where is set out the many stigmatised, provincial status, [əi]-type realisations of the historical [ɔi] diphthong (spelt ‹i›) provided by Kirkham (1833) and Humphreys (1815), against instances of lexical items etymologically containing [ɔi] as they appear in the settlers' letters:

Kirkham		*Humphreys*		*Settlers' letters*	
[əi]/[ai]		[əi]/[ai]		[ɔi]	[əi]
‹pint›	'*point*'	‹viges›	'*voyages*'	‹adjoining› (37)	
‹kwite›	'*quite*'	‹lines›	'*loins*'	‹appointed› (23)	‹apinted› (7)
‹histe›	'*hoist*'	‹briled›	'*broiled*'	‹apointed› (37)	
‹ile›	'*oil*'	‹ile›		‹Oppointed› (28)	
‹bile›	'*boil*'	‹bile›		‹joine› (34)	
				‹joines› (22)	
				‹Disappointments› (27)	
				‹disappointed› (27)	

Quite remarkably, the Sierra Leone letters show but one instance of what the other American grammarians note to be the socially stigmatised [əi] pronunciation – ‹apinted› '*appointed*' (Document 7). Now we might not wish to treat this single piece of evidence at its face value, arguing instead that ‹oi› spellings were used by our writers in the formal context of the epistle, their speech showing the [əɪ] and not [ɔɪ] shape in all the above items. But many of the ‹oi› spellings are to be found in letters (notably Documents 27, 28, 34, 37) where the density of non-standard spelling forms is high and it would be perverse to suggest [ɔɪ]-containing items were being used there as the salient marker of written medium formality.

We might just take these ‹oi› spellings at their face value and argue that [əɪ] for [ɔɪ] was not a marked characteristic of the phonology of these Nova Scotian speakers and that such a feature made them stand out against other contemporary 'provincial' and 'improper' United States speakers who are recorded as using the [əɪ] diphthong.

CONSONANTAL EFFECTS

Cluster reduction and simplification

The spellings in the settlers' letters point to several interesting characteristics of late eighteenth-century consonantal behaviour although, as we shall see, phonological explanation for such phenomena are complex. One of the most recurrent features of the letter writers' orthography is its tendency to produce idiosyncratic outputs for sequences of clusters of consonantal segments, especially at syllable terminations. Consider the following:

‹superintended›	*'superintendent'*	(24)
‹Confidence›	*'confident'*	(27)
‹convenence›	*'convenient'*	(33)

The terminating syllables of these items show what appears to be a motley collection of segment deletions, resulting in cluster simplifications such that [dɛnt] → [dɛd], [dɛnt] → [dɛns] and [jɛnt] → [jɛns]. The last three instances suggest a syllable final cluster alternation like [nts]~[ns], one reflected (in 'reverse') by spellings like ‹pends› for ‹pence› *'pence'* (Document 32), ‹present› *'presence'* (Document 14) and perhaps ‹excellents› *'excellent'* (Document 13). Such an alternation points to what phonologists see as a syllable final 'strengthening', whereby consonantal quality is suppressed in favour of increased relative vocalicness in that context. In the cases above, the suppression of the dental obstruent ([d]/[t]) realises a cluster [ns] showing more pronounced vocalic characteristics (sonorant + fricative), a phenomenon also probably the motivation behind a spelling like ‹Fruth› *'fruit'* (Document 34) with its substitution of a more vowel-like fricative [θ] for the maximally consonantal voiceless [t] segment (Lass, 1984: pp. 177 ff). That such cluster simplifications were a contemporary and stigmatised feature of the phonology can be deduced from Jackson's (1830: p. 18) condemnations of (munce) pronunciations for (months) *'months'* (cf. Humphrey's ‹close› *'clothes'*).

Such considerations also perhaps underlie the [st]~[s] alternation we find in ‹greates› *'greatest'* (Document 33) and ‹sarvast› *'service'* (Document 33) (but note ‹Repect› *'respect'*: Document 34). Yet not all cluster alternations can be explained in such a fashion (however informally expressed here) and a more detailed study would be required to handle the significance of realisations such as ‹presst› *'present'* (Document 33), ‹compy› *'comply'* (Document 32), ‹nuber› *'number'* (Document 32), ‹actr› *'acre'* (Document 36) and ‹nont› *'not'* (Document 33), and several others.

Metathesis

Manifest throughout the history of the English language and a common feature in the modern language (cf. such language acquisitional mis-processings as [ægɪleitə] *'alligator'* and [ɛfələnt] *'elephant'* (Jones, 1980)) the transposition of consonantal segments around the syllable peak is a process for which there is some evidence in the settlers' letters. The majority of such transpositions in the history of the English language appear to involve an [r] segment, and we commonly find alternants such as ‹frost›/‹forst› *'frost'*, ‹thrid›/‹third› *'third'* and ‹crudde›/‹curd› *'cheese'* at most periods of the language's evolution (Jones, 1989: pp. 190 ff.). Both Humphreys and Sherwood record such types (as stigmatised) but there seems to be only one possible instance in the settlers' letters (‹Ezerlites› *'Isrealites'*, Document 30), which otherwise show a less common type of metathesis more like that we mentioned at the beginning of this section:

Humphreys	*Sherwood*	*Settlers' letters*
‹pertection›	‹pervision›	‹Phemplet›
‹pertest›	‹perserves›	‹Relusution›
‹prehaps›	‹perdigious›	
	‹prevade›	
	‹thrust› *'thirst'*	

In the settlers' letters, orthographic shapes such as ‹Phemplet› *'pamphlet'* (Document 34) and certainly ‹Relusution› *'resolution'* (Document 37) – cf. ‹Rasalition› (Document 12) – suggest alternations such as [pæmf]~[fɛmp] and [zəl]~[ləz], where a syllable initial element relatively low in vowel-ness value is substituted for one with a higher value, although for a more detailed argumentation for the motivation for such a process the reader is referred to Jones (1989: pp. 190–96). That it was seen as non-standard, even stigmatised, might be inferred from Jackson's (1830: pp. 16–24) injunction against pronunciations like (irrevelant) *'irrelevant'*, (progidy) *'prodigy'*, (palarytic) *'paralytic'*, (renumerate) *'remunerate'*, and (tradegy) *'tragedy'*. Yet the apparent absence of [r] metathesis from the settlers' letters is interesting, suggesting that unlike many contemporary English variants, the process had no sociolinguistic significance.

Word initial [hw]~[w] alternations

Modern British English speakers are familiar with the regional contrast between word initial [hw–] and [w–] in items like ‹who›, ‹what›, ‹when›, etc., speakers from northern parts of the country generally favouring the former, the unaspirated version having a generally southern provenance as well as marking 'standard' usage (Wells, 1982: pp. 228–30). The data from our letters suggest that perhaps both types were known to their authors, although we might just interpret the ‹wh–› spellings as residual orthographic marks, the phonetics mostly realising [w–], thus:

‹wane›	*'when'*	(22)
‹wich›	*'which'*	(22)
‹witbread›	*'Whitbread'*	(32)
‹wheather›	*'whether'*	(26)
‹where›	*'were'*	(1)

[n]/[ŋ] variables

Perhaps one of the most obvious markers of informal English world-wide is the tendency to substitute a dental for a velar nasal syllable finally, as in the [meɪkɪn]/[meɪkɪŋ] *'making'* alternation. Yet, as can be seen from the following data, the distribution of the [n]/[ŋ] variation is not simply one of level of formality or social class, but involves other factors as well. Consider the following data from Sherwood's *Provincialisms* and Kirkham's *New England/New York Provincialisms* alongside those from the settlers' letters:

Sherwood		Kirkham		Settlers' letters	
1		‹goin›	*'going'*	‹shillens›	*'shillings'* (7)
		‹geestin›	*'jesting'*	‹haven›	*'having'* (7)
		‹jokin›	*'joking'*	‹a Coarden›	*'according'* (7)
				‹undertaken›	*'–taking'* (7)
				‹goin›	*'going'* (14)
				‹marain›	*'marrying'* (16)
2		‹cissing›	*'kissing'*		
		‹pairsing›	*'parsing'*		
3					
‹brethering›	*'brothers'*			‹benge›	*'been'* (14)
‹Capting›	*'captain'*			‹being›	*'been'* (7)
‹garding›	*'garden'*				
‹mounting›	*'mountain'*				

Some interesting points arise from these data. In the first place, Kirkham's evidence suggests that while [n] terminations

are non-standard, even in provincial dialects [ŋ] will surface
(as in ‹cissing› and ‹pairsing›), the [ŋ] → [n] change being a
feature of an identifiable set of lexical items; other items, like
‹pairsing› and ‹cissing› are (often) non-responsive to the
develarisation process. This phenomenon is known as *lexical
diffusion* and full details of its operation can be found in Wang
(1969). Secondly, both the settlers' letters and Sherwood
show instances under (³) where [ŋ] forms are used 'unetymo-
logically' (indeed, Sherwood appears to show only such
forms). Perhaps what we are witnessing here are instances of
'hypercorrection', the syllable terminal [n] being so stigmatised that speakers tend to substitute [ŋ] shapes even in
contexts where they would not lexically/morphologically be
expected to surface (Trudgill, 1986).

Observations not unlike these may also be appropriate to
the fairly common syllable final [nd]/[n] alternation which
also appears at most historical periods of the English language. Consider the following:

Humphreys		Sherwood		Settlers' letters	
1					
‹hansum›	*'handsome'*			‹secon›	*'second'* (7)
‹stan›	*'stand'*			‹govern›	*'governed'* (7)
				‹hen›	*'hand'* (7)
				‹sining›	*'sending'* (33)
2					
		‹beyont›	*'beyond'*		
		‹holt›	*'hold'*		
3					
‹gownd›	*'gown'*	‹sarment›	*'sermon'*		
		‹varment›	*'vermin'*		
		‹yont›	*'yonder'*		

While we may accept the [d] effaced items under (¹) as
representative of non-standard/stigmatised pronunciation at
the close of the eighteenth and beginning of the nineteenth
centuries, it is interesting to observe once more the 'hyper-
correct' ‹gownd›; again, while Sherwood's data suggest that

syllable final devoicing of [d] → [t] was 'provincial', his forms under (³) perhaps hint that the devoiced termination was spreading across the entire lexicon to the extent that it was seen as the appropriate 'hypercorrected' shape.

The above by no means exhaust the indications of contemporary pronunciation from the idiosyncratic spelling conventions of the authors of the settlers' letters. Realisations like ‹tegus› *'tedious'* (Document 32), ‹Religus› *'religious'* (Document 15) as against ‹Colledge› *'college'* (Document 20) perhaps suggest [tidjəs] rather than the later [tidʒəs] type pronunciation, while those in ‹lov› *'love'* (Document 33), ‹ous› *'us'* (Document 34) and ‹toung› *'tongue'* (Document 25) may just possibly indicate that the historical [u] in such words was coming to show the lower and more central [ə]/[ʌ] pronunciation characteristic of much 'standard' British English speech. Again, spellings such as ‹mushel› *'muzzle'* (Document 34), ‹proposhall›, ‹proposhals› *'proposal(s)'* (Document 25), ‹parshige› *'passage'* (Document 14), ‹Philish› *'Phillis'* (Document 14) point to some kind of (intervocalic) fricativisation such that [z] → [š] – cf. Jackson's (1830) strictures against (nonplush'd) *'non-plussed'* and (overplush) *'overplus'* (also recorded by Sherwood). But a full exemplification of the orthographic/phonetic correpondences of these letters is beyond the scope of a short paper such as this, and we have left unexplained a whole set of suggestive orthographic shapes such as ‹reasnenble› (Document 7) *'reasonable'*, ‹consirent› (Document 7) *'consistent'*, ‹sighn› (Document 12) *'sign'* and ‹New Brumswick› (Document 15).

SYNTACTIC PECULIARITIES OF THE SIERRA LEONE SETTLERS' LETTERS

While any comment upon the syntactic characteristics of our letters must await a full analysis of their discourse and stylistic peculiarities, we can nevertheless point to at least two areas in the syntax/morphology where usage is markedly at variance with contemporary prestigious prose writing. Most notably, our writers very often show no congruence, agreement markers for number between nouns and their sentential predicates: plural subjects trigger singular verb shapes and (less commonly) singular subjects show verbs more appropriate for plural contexts in standard writing habits. Consider the following:

¹ the Rains is now set in (19)
² he does so many things which seems to us (19)
³ The times is not as it was (23)
⁴ Your honours very well knows (25)
⁵ But God have spared me (22)
⁶ The Protector of these articles have a just Right (24)

Again, the construction traditionally known as the 'past participle' (the aspectual marker of completed state activity) shows three peculiarities. In the first place, the main verb is realised with its ‹ed› suffix effaced:

¹ Your Hon^d... have sheaw the same affection (34)
² I have precur you one of the Governor Pmphle (33)
³ thay was a great many proboshalls propose by Mr McCawly (25)
⁴ the French have Attacked us and Destroy all the Compy Property (24)

Secondly, in such constructions, the auxiliary ‹have› verb can itself be effaced, as in:

¹ it would long ago been fulfilled (27)
² they mought took the place (28)
³ it should been Return (26)
⁴ all the wrongs which are Done to us here since we been (36)

Thirdly, the main verb shape is one we no longer normally associate with 'past participle' contexts:

¹ we have most humbly took upon ourselves (26)
² the Hat I have gave to Mr Domingo (33)

[3] we have bore our hardships a long time (19)
[4] And hoving now find we are oppressed (36)

while such verbal constructions like ‹as many as I was dare to show your letter› (Document 33) and ‹how much More is your Hon[d] ought to be Estemed› (Document 34) are clearly of a markedly non-standard type. It is difficult to see how one could argue for a purely pidgin/creole source for any of these syntactic/morphological realisations. 'Irregularities' involving number congruence marking and main verb morphological depletion in complex verbal constructions are hardly confined to such linguistic specialisms, but are the commonplace of regional and historical mutation.

There is, indeed, little in the settlers' letters to suggest that they were composed by speakers whose English was of either a simple or advanced pidgin type. On the contrary, we have tried to demonstrate that the language of these letters represents a kind well attested for contemporary American and British native English speakers, possibly of the lower social orders. Other than the retention of post-vocalic [r], the lack of [r] metathesis and the non-conflation of the [ɔɪ]/[əɪ] diphthongs, there seems to be no indication in the letters of features which might unambiguously be described as unique to speakers who were Nova Scotian, black or of African origin, however distant.

REFERENCES

Alleyne, M. C. (1974) *Comparative Afro-American*, Ann Arbor: Karoma

Bartsch, R. (1987) *Norms of Language: Theoretical and Practical Aspects*, London: Longman

Berndt, R. (1960) *Einführung in das Studium des Mittelenglischen*, Halle: Niemeyer

Cade, J. B. (1935) 'Out of the mouths of ex-slaves', *Journal of Negro History* 20, 294–337

Combs, J. H. (1916) 'Old, early and Elizabethan English in the southern mountains', *Dialect Notes* 4, 283–97

Cruikshank, J. G. (1910) *Black Talk: Being Notes on Negro Dialect in British Guiana*, Demarara

Dillard, J. L. (1971) 'The history of Black English in Nova Scotia – a first step', *African Language Review* 9, 263–79

────── (1972) 'On the beginnings of black English in the New World', *Orbis* 21, 523–36

────── (1973) *Black English: Its History and Usage in the United States*, New York: Vintage Books

────── (1985) *Toward a Social History of American English*, The Hague: Mouton

Dobson, E. J. (1968) *English Pronunciation 1500–1700*, Oxford: Oxford University Press

Ekwall, E. (1975) *A History of Modern English Sounds and Morphology*, Oxford: Blackwell

Hancock, I. (1986) 'The domestic hypothesis, diffusion and componentiality: an account of Atlantic Anglophone Creole origins', in P. Muysken and N. Smith (eds) *Substrata vs. Universals in Creole Genesis*, Amsterdam: John Benjamins, 71–103

Harris, J. (1985) *Phonological Variation and Change: Studies in Hiberno English*, Cambridge: Cambridge University Press

Jackson, G. (1830) *Popular Errors of English Grammar Particularly of Pronunciation*, London: Effingham Wilson

Jones, C. (1980) 'Some characteristics of sonorant–obstruent metathesis within a dependency framework', in J. M. Anderson and C. J. Ewen (eds) *Studies in Dependency Phonology*, Lüdwigsburg Studies in Language and Linguistics 4, Lüdwigsburg 139–55

────── (1989) *A History of English Phonology*, London: Longman

Kirkham, S. (1833) *English Grammar in Familiar Lectures*, Rochester, NY: Marshall and Dean

Kökevitz, H. (1944) *Mather Flint in Early Eighteenth-Century Pronunciation*, Uppsala: Almqvist.

Lass, R. (1984) *Phonology: An Introduction to Basic Concepts*, Cambridge: Cambridge University Press

Lowell, J. R. (1880) *The Biglow Papers*, London: Trübner

Mather, J. Y. and H. H. Speitel (1986) *The Linguistic Atlas of Scotland, Scots Section, Volume III, Phonology*, London: Croom Helm

Mathews, M. M. (1931) *The Beginnings of American English: Essays and Comments*, Chicago: University of Chicago Press

Matthews, W. (1936a) 'William Tiffin, an eighteenth century phonetician', *English Studies* 18, 97–114

————— (1936b) 'Some eighteenth century phonetic spellings', *English Studies* 12, 47–60, 177–188

Nichols, J. G. (1848) *The Diary of Henry Machyn, Citizen and Merchant-Taylor of London*, Camden Society, 42, London

Ohala, J. J. (1974) 'Experimental historical phonology', in J. M. Anderson and C. Jones *Historical Linguistics II*, Amsterdam: North Holland, 353–89

Orbeck, A. (1927) *Early New England Pronunciation*, Michigan: Ann Arbor

Osselton, N. E. (1977) *The Dumb Linguists*, Leiden: Leiden U P

Read, A. W. (1933) 'British recognition of American speech in the eighteenth century', *Dialect Notes* 6, 313–34

Trudgill, P. (1986) *Dialects in Contact*, Oxford: Blackwell

Vachek, J. (1973) *Written Language: General Problems and Problems of English*, The Hague: Mouton

Verney, F. P. and M. M. Verney (1925) *Memoirs of the Verney family*, London: Coates.

Walker, J. (1791) *A Critical Pronouncing Dictionary and Expositor of the English Language*, R. C. Alston (ed.) (1968) *English Linguistics 1500–1800*, Menston: The Scholar Press

Wang, W. (1969) 'Competing changes as a cause of rasidue', *Language* 45, 9–25

Wells, J. C. (1982) *Accents of English*, Cambridge: Cambridge University Press

Wyld, H. C. (1936) *A History of Modern Colloquial English*, Oxford: Blackwell

Zachrisson, R. E. (1913) *Pronunciation of English Vowels 1400–1700*, Göteborgs Kungl. Vetenskaps. och vitterhetssamhälks handlingar, 14, no. 2, Göteborg

Selected Bibliography

Cox-George, N. A. *Finance and Development in Africa: The Sierra Leone Experience*, London, 1961

Fyfe, Christopher *A History of Sierra Leone*, London, 1962

Hunter, Yema Lucilda *Road to Freedom*, Ibadan, 1982

Kup, Alexander Peter (ed.) *Adam Afzelius Sierra Leone Journal*, Uppsala, 1967

Peterson, John *Province of Freedom*, London, 1969

Porter, Arthur T. *Creoledom*, Oxford, 1963

Walker, James W. St. G. *The Black Loyalists*, London, 1976

Wilson, Ellen Gibson *The Loyal Blacks*, New York, 1976

———*John Clarkson and the African Adventure*, London, 1980